Easy Microsoft® Office 97

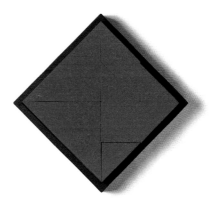

Trudi Reisner

Easy Microsoft® Office 97

Library of Congress Catalog Card Number: 96-71447

International Standard Book Number: 0-7897-1078-1

99 98 97   8 7 6 5 4 3 2

Interpretation of the printing code: the rightmost double-digit number is the year of the book's first printing; the rightmost single-digit number is the number of the book's printing. For example, a printing code of 97-1 shows that this copy of the book was printed during the first printing of the book in 1997.

Screen reproductions in this book were created by means of the program Collage Complete from Inner Media, Inc, Hollis, NH.

Printed in the United States of America

Dedication

To remarkable Kim Cohen

Credits

Publisher
Roland Elgey

Publishing Manager
Lynn E. Zingraf

Editorial Services Director
Elizabeth Keaffaber

Managing Editor
Michael Cunningham

Director of Marketing
Lynn E. Zingraf

Acquisitions Editor
Martha O'Sullivan

Technical Specialist
Nadeem Muhammed

Product Development Specialists
Lorna Gentry
Nancy Warner

Technical Editor
Kyle Bryant

Production Editor
Audra Gable

Copy Editors
Geneil Breeze
Kate Givens

Book Designers
Barbara Kordesh
Ruth Harvey

Cover Designers
Dan Armstrong
Kim Scott

Production Team
Tammy Ahrens
Toi Davis
Sean Decker
Brad Dixon
Tammy Graham
Stephanie Hammett
Jason Hand
Daniel Harris
Deb Kincaid
Pete Lippincott
Kevin J. MacDonald
Erich Richter
Laura Robbins
Bryan Towse
Marvin
  Van Tiem

Indexers
Cheryl Dietsch
CJ East

Composed in *Syntax* and *New Century Schoolbook* by Que Corporation

We'd Like to Hear from You!

As part of our continuing effort to produce books of the highest possible quality, Que would like to hear your comments. To stay competitive, we *really* want you, as a computer book reader and user, to let us know what you like or dislike most about this book or other Que products.

You can mail comments, ideas, or suggestions for improving future editions to the address below, or send us a fax at (317) 581-4663. For the online inclined, Macmillan Computer Publishing has a forum on CompuServe (type **GO QUEBOOKS** at any prompt) through which our staff and authors are available for questions and comments. The address of our Internet site is **http://www.mcp.com/que** (World Wide Web).

In addition to exploring our forum, please feel free to contact me personally to discuss your opinions of this book: I'm **75703,3251** on CompuServe, and I'm **lgentry@que.mcp.com** on the Internet.

Although we cannot provide general technical support, we're happy to help you resolve problems you encounter related to our books, disks, or other products. If you need such assistance, please contact our Tech Support department at 800-545-5914 ext. 3833.

To order other Que or Macmillan Computer Publishing books or products, please call our Customer Service department at 800-835-3202 ext. 666.

Thanks in advance—your comments will help us to continue publishing the best books available on computer topics in today's market.

Lorna Gentry
Product Development Specialist
Que Corporation
201 West 103rd St.
Indianapolis, Indiana 46290
USA

About the Author

Trudi Reisner is a computer technical writer specializing in software technical writing and course development. Trudi has written numerous books including Que's *10 Minute Guide to Excel 5*, *10 Minute Guide to Windows 95*, *Easy Excel 5 for Windows*, *Easy Microsoft Office*, *Easy Word for Windows 95*, *Excel VisiRef*, and *Windows 3.11 VisiRef*. Trudi has also written user guides on manufacturing, clinical and financial, and font creation software, as well as courseware on Lotus 1-2-3 and Lotus Notes Web Navigator.

Acknowledgments

My warmest thanks to Martha O'Sullivan, Acquisitions Editor at Que, who gave me the opportunity to write this book; Nancy Warner, the Development Editor who helped develop the content and gave excellent suggestions; Kyle Bryant, Technical Editor, who technically reviewed the final draft; Audra Gable, Geneil Breeze, and Kate Givens who tirelessly managed the author review process and edited the manuscript; and the production staff for producing and proofreading the entire book. As always, it was a pleasure to work with all of you.

Finally, thanks to Microsoft Corporation, who developed and produced a superb integrated program.

Trademarks

Contents

Part IV: Formatting Text in Word — 85

Part V: Viewing and Printing the Word Document — 115

Part VI: Entering and Editing Data in Excel — 127

Part VII: Working with Formulas — 171

Contents

Part XI: Using Microsoft Office and the World Wide Web 281

Index 298

Introduction

What You Can Do with Microsoft Office 97

Microsoft Office contains three of the world's most popular software products on the market today: Microsoft Word, Microsoft Excel, and Microsoft PowerPoint. In addition to Word, Excel, and PowerPoint, Office provides Outlook, the added functionality to working with the World Wide Web, and the Office integration capabilities.

Although you could create documents on a typewriter, Word makes writing, editing, and printing easier. Likewise, you could create worksheets on ledger paper and use a calculator, or you could draw charts on graph paper, but Excel makes managing numeric information easier. You can use Excel to create worksheets, databases, charts, and macros.

Microsoft PowerPoint can help you with your whole presentation. You can create professional-looking visual aids, such as overheads or 35mm slides, and you can plan and organize speeches.

Microsoft Outlook is a personal information manager that can organize and manage your e-mail, faxes, tasks and projects, business and personal contacts, appointments and events, and meetings.

Microsoft Office enables you to browse the World Wide Web and publish Office documents as Web pages. Not only is the World Wide Web integrated with Office, but all the software programs within Microsoft Office are fully integrated—which can help make your "Office" competitive with technology.

Specifically, you can use Microsoft Word to perform these functions:

- *Correct errors.* When you type on a typewriter, after you press a key, that letter is committed to paper. To correct a mistake, you have to use a corrector (such as Whiteout) or retype the document. With Microsoft Word, you see the data on-screen, and you can correct any typographical errors easily before you print the document.

- *Move around quickly.* With the document on-screen, you can move from one sentence, paragraph, or page to another. You can move quickly from the top of the document to the bottom and vice versa.

- *Make editing changes.* You can insert text into any location in your document. You can also delete any amount of text quickly, such as a character, a word, a sentence, a paragraph, or a block of text.

- *Rearrange your text.* When you sit down to write, you don't always write in order from the introduction to the summary. Ideas may occur to you in a different order. As you're writing the summary, you might think of an idea that belongs in the introduction. With Microsoft Word, you can easily move and copy data from one location to another.

- *Restore deleted text.* When you accidentally delete data that you want to keep, you don't have to retype it. Instead, you can just restore the data.

- *Check spelling.* Before you print, you can run a spell check to search for misspellings and double words. If you are a poor typist, this feature enables you to concentrate on your writing and leave spelling errors for Microsoft Word to catch.

- *Search for text.* You can search your document for a particular word or phrase. For example, you can move quickly to the section of your document that discusses expenditures by searching for the word "expenditures."

- *Search and replace text.* You can make text replacements throughout the document quickly and easily. For example, you can change all occurrences of the name "Smith" to "Smythe" in a document.

- *Make formatting changes.* Word enables you to change margins, tabs, and other formatting options easily. You can experiment with the settings until the document appears the way that you want it. Then you can print it.

- *Change how text is printed.* You can make text bold, italic, and underlined. You can also use a different typeface (depending on your printer).

- *Preview your document.* You can preview your document to see how it will look when you print it. If you want to make changes before you print, you can do this when you return to normal view.

You can use Microsoft Excel to perform these functions:

- *Lay out a worksheet.* When you sit down to develop a worksheet with a pencil and ledger paper, you don't always have all the information to complete the design and layout of the worksheet. Ideas may occur to you after you sketch the layout of your worksheet. For example, after you're finished jotting down the column headings and the row headings, you might think of another column or row you didn't include. With Excel, you can insert columns and rows easily and move data from one location to another.

- *Calculate numbers.* If you have a checkbook register, you subtract the amount of each check written and add the deposits to the running balance. When you receive your bank statement and balance your checkbook, you might find that you made math errors in your checkbook. In this case, you must erase the old answers, recalculate the numbers, and jot down the new answers. In Excel, you enter a formula once. Then, when you change the numbers in the worksheet, Excel recalculates the formulas instantly and gives you the new answers.

- *Make editing changes.* To correct a mistake on ledger paper, you have to either use an eraser or reconstruct the entire worksheet. With Excel, you can overwrite data in any cell in your worksheet. You can also delete data quickly—in one cell or a range of cells.

- *Undo mistakes.* When you accidentally delete data that you want to keep, you don't have to retype it. Instead, you can just restore the data with the Undo feature. You can also use the Undo command to reverse the last command or action.

- *Check spelling.* Before you print, you can run a spell check to search for misspellings. If you are a poor typist, this feature enables you to concentrate on calculating your numbers and leaves catching spelling errors for Excel.

- *Make formatting changes.* Excel easily enables you to align data in cells; center column headings across columns; adjust column widths; display numbers with dollar signs, commas, and decimal points; and apply other formatting options. You can experiment with the settings until the worksheet appears the way that you want it. Then you can print it.

- *Change how data is printed.* You can make data bold, italic, and underlined. Excel also lets you shade cells and add borders. And you can use a different typeface (depending on your printer).

- *Preview your print job.* You can preview your worksheet to see how it will look when you print it. If you want to make changes before you print, you can do this in print preview also.

- *Chart numeric data.* You can track the sales trends of several products with an embedded column chart. Make as many "what if?" projections as you want in the worksheet by increasing and decreasing the numbers. As you change the numbers in the worksheet, Excel instantly updates the embedded chart. Excel's embedded charts let you view simultaneously the sales trends in a picture representation on-screen and the numbers in the worksheet, making your sales forecasting more efficient.

You can use Microsoft PowerPoint to perform these functions:

- *Create visual aids.* You can create overheads or 35mm slides to build your whole slide show presentation from beginning to end.

- *Plan and organize your speech.* You can use the outline feature to outline your speech, lay out your main ideas, and organize your presentation.

- *Create speaker's notes.* PowerPoint lets you create speaker's notes that you can take with you to the podium.

- *Use predefined presentations.* You can use the built-in wizards to quickly and easily create a new presentation. When you create a presentation, the AutoContent Wizard enables you to choose from several well-designed presentation outlines that you can modify.

- *Add graphs to your presentation.* With Microsoft Graph, a business graph program, you can add great-looking graphs to your presentation. You just type your data in place of the sample data that Graph provides. Graph does the work for you—all you need to do is choose the correct graph type for your data!

Microsoft Outlook is a personal information manager program in Microsoft Office that you can use to do the following:

- *Send and receive e-mail messages.* You can use the Inbox to send and receive messages and faxes. You can preview your messages in the Preview box, create a new message, attach a file to a message, and reply to an incoming message.

- *Create a daily schedule.* The Calendar enables you to schedule appointments and events. A reminder bell sounds an alert to remind you when your appointment or event is going to happen. You can display your schedule in a daily, weekly, or monthly view. Calendar also helps you plan a meeting by inviting attendees, determining a meeting time, and assigning a location.

- *Create a To Do List.* You can create tasks for a project and then track and monitor them using The Do List. The TaskPad can show you all the tasks involved in the project, today's tasks to be done, tasks that need to be done in the next seven days, and overdue tasks.

- *Create a Contacts list.* You can create a Contacts list to store names, addresses, and phone numbers for business and personal contacts. The Contacts list enables you to quickly find contact information, dial a contact's phone and fax, and use the addresses for Mail Merge letters.

- *Create a journal.* You can record mail messages, documents, contact information, notes, or any information that you want to store and then review it at any time. You can document many of the actions that you perform in Office.

- *Create notes.* You can create electronic sticky notes that contain reminders, directions, instructions, or any other notes that you would write on note paper.

You can use Microsoft Office to perform these functions:

- *Publish Web pages.* You can convert a Word document, an Excel worksheet data and chart, and a PowerPoint presentation into HTML format. Then you can publish the HTML document as a Web page on the World Wide Web.

- *Browse the Web*. With Office's Web toolbar, you can browse the Web, move backward and forward among open Web pages, refresh the current Web page, and store your favorite Web pages in the Favorite Places folder.

- *Create a hyperlink to move between Office documents*. You can create a hyperlink in a Word document to move to a spreadsheet in Excel. The hyperlink contains the document path and appears in a color in the Word document. You click the hyperlink to move to the Excel spreadsheet.

- *Insert an Excel spreadsheet into a Word document*. You can create a document in Word and create a spreadsheet in Excel, and then use the Copy and Paste commands to insert the spreadsheet into the Word document.

- *Insert clip art into a Word document*. You can easily insert a Word ClipArt picture that comes with the Word program into a Word document. That way, you don't have to leave the Word program. You also don't have to draw a picture in another program and insert the clip art with any complicated procedure.

- *Insert an Excel chart into a Word document*. You can easily insert an Excel chart into a Word document. Charts can spice up an annual report and clearly illustrate a particular point you want to make. Instead of inserting a table or worksheet that contains numbers, try using an Excel chart to express an idea—it makes the data easier to understand.

Part Sections

The Part sections introduce each part and list the tasks included in the part. If you are already familiar with a part, you can read the paragraphs in the part section and go on, or you can read the introductory paragraphs to become familiar with the information that you are going to go through with each task to become efficient.

Task Sections

The Task sections include numbered steps that tell you how to accomplish certain tasks, such as saving a document or indenting a paragraph. The numbered steps walk you through a specific example so that you can learn the task by doing it.

Big Screen

At the beginning of each task is a large screen that shows how the computer screen will look either after you complete the procedure in that task or at some key point during the task.

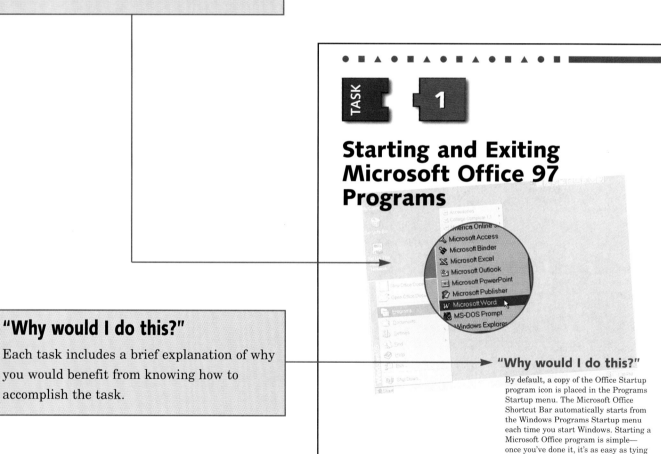

TASK 1

Starting and Exiting Microsoft Office 97 Programs

- Microsoft Access
- Microsoft Binder
- Microsoft Excel
- Microsoft Outlook
- Microsoft PowerPoint
- Microsoft Publisher
- Microsoft Word
- MS-DOS Prompt
- Windows Explorer

"Why would I do this?"

Each task includes a brief explanation of why you would benefit from knowing how to accomplish the task.

"Why would I do this?"

By default, a copy of the Office Startup program icon is placed in the Programs Startup menu. The Microsoft Office Shortcut Bar automatically starts from the Windows Programs Startup menu each time you start Windows. Starting a Microsoft Office program is simple—once you've done it, it's as easy as tying your shoe! When you no longer want to work in a Microsoft Office program, you can exit the program and return to the Windows desktop.

6

Step-by-Step Screens

Each task includes a screen shot for each step of a procedure. The screen shot shows how the computer screen will look at each step in the process.

Task 1: Starting and Exiting Microsoft Office 97 Programs

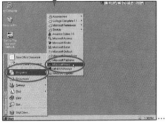

1 Open the **Start** menu, choose **Programs**, and select **Microsoft Word**. This starts the Word program.

Missing Link

To instantly create a new document or open an existing document, click the **New Office Document** button or the **Open Office Document** button on the Office Shortcut Bar.

Missing Link Notes

Many tasks contain other short notes that tell you a little more about certain procedures. These notes define terms, explain other options, refer you to other sections when applicable, and so on.

2 A blank document appears in a window on-screen. (Each time you start the program, the startup screen with your name and the Microsoft license agreement appears before the blank document.)

Puzzled? Notes

You may find that you performed a task that you didn't want to do after all. The Puzzled? notes tell you how to undo certain procedures or get out of a situation you didn't mean to get into.

3 Click **File** in the menu bar. This selects the File command and opens the File menu. You see a list of File commands. Click **Exit**. This selects the Exit command. You return to the Windows desktop. ■

Puzzled?

To close a menu without making a selection, press the **Esc** key or click anywhere outside of the menu.

7

PART
I

The Basics

▲ ● ■ ▲ ● ■ ▲ ●

PART 1 INTRODUCES you to Microsoft Office basics. You need to know some fundamental things about Microsoft Office before you start working with the Microsoft Office applications and creating your own documents.

In this part, you learn how to start and exit Microsoft Office programs. You should make sure that Microsoft Office is installed on your hard disk so that it appears in your Windows Programs menu. To install Microsoft Office, follow the installation instructions on disk and on-screen. You can start and exit Microsoft Office and any of its applications as you would any Windows application.

When you start Microsoft Office, the program may display the Microsoft Office Shortcut Bar (depending upon the type of Microsoft Office installation), located in the upper-right corner of your screen. This toolbar contains buttons for creating a new Office document, opening an Office document, and using Microsoft Outlook's features that include setting an appointment, making a journal entry, sending e-mail, and creating a contact list, a to do list, and a note.

The tasks in this part are common to all Microsoft Office applications. You learn how to perform these tasks in Microsoft Word; however, you can perform these tasks the same way in Excel and PowerPoint.

When you start Word, you see a blank document—much like a blank piece of paper. The document is a file in which you store your data. When you start Excel, the program displays the first worksheet of a blank workbook. The workbook is a file in which you store your data, similar to a three-ring binder filled with ledger paper. When you start PowerPoint, you see a dialog box for creating a new presentation or opening an existing presentation.

In all three programs, the *menu bar* is located directly below the title bar. This menu bar contains pull-down menus for commands. A *toolbar* appears below the menu bar that contains buttons for common commands and provides quick access to commands you use frequently. You learn how to use the Word toolbar. Each program ships with many different toolbars that include the tools you use for formatting text, drawing graphics, creating macros, and many other operations. Sometimes you might want to have a clean screen or you may want to make more rows in a document visible. You can hide the toolbars to make more room on-screen.

In this part, you are shown how to view toolbar *ScreenTips* (the toolbar button names). The toolbar ScreenTips feature displays the button names for each button on the toolbar.

The *text area* is the large empty space beneath the toolbars; this is where you enter the text of your document. The *insertion point* is a flashing vertical bar that appears in the text area. Text that you type appears at the insertion point. A horizontal line at the end of the text area is called the *end mark*. When you position the mouse pointer inside the text area, the mouse pointer appears as an I-beam, a thin vertical icon in the shape of the letter I.

In this part, you learn how to use the shortcut menus. When you point to text in Word, or a single cell or a selected range of cells in Excel, or an object in PowerPoint and then click the right mouse button, you see a shortcut menu. This menu appears next to the text, cell, or selected range of cells. Shortcut menus contain fewer commands than a menu in the menu bar. The commands on the shortcut menus vary, depending on the text, cells, or object you select in the document or worksheet. You might find it quicker and easier to use a shortcut menu than to select commands from the menu bar and the pull-down menus.

This part also discusses some of the ways you can get help in Office. You can get instant online Help and tips for many operations with the Office Assistant. Help in Excel, PowerPoint, and Outlook closely resemble Help in Word.

Starting and Exiting Microsoft Office 97 Programs

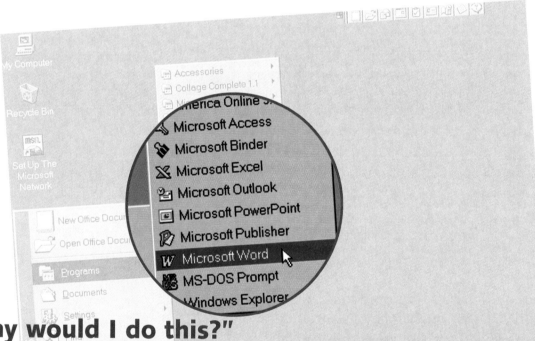

"Why would I do this?"

By default, a copy of the Office Startup program icon is placed in the Programs Startup menu. The Microsoft Office Shortcut Bar automatically starts from the Windows Programs Startup menu each time you start Windows. Starting a

Microsoft Office program is simple—once you've done it, it's as easy as tying your shoe! When you no longer want to work in a Microsoft Office program, you can exit the program and return to the Windows desktop.

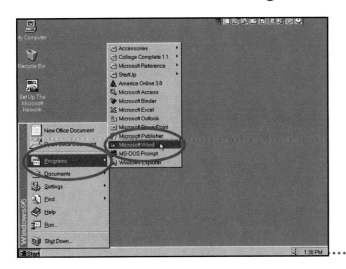

1 Open the **Start** menu, choose **Programs**, and select **Microsoft Word**. This starts the Word program.

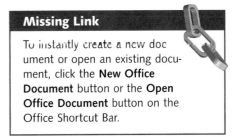

Missing Link

To instantly create a new document or open an existing document, click the **New Office Document** button or the **Open Office Document** button on the Office Shortcut Bar.

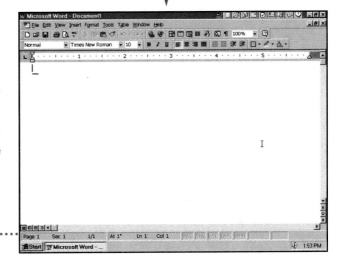

2 A blank document appears in a window on-screen. (Each time you start the program, the startup screen with your name and the Microsoft license agreement appears before the blank document.)

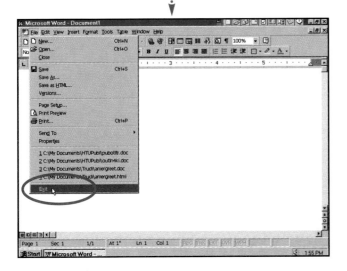

3 Click **File** in the menu bar. This selects the File command and opens the File menu. You see a list of File commands. Click **Exit**. This selects the Exit command. You return to the Windows desktop. ■

Selecting a Menu Command

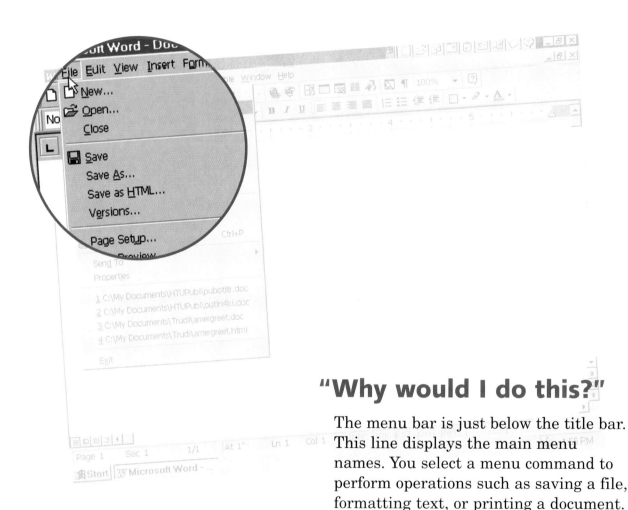

"Why would I do this?"

The menu bar is just below the title bar. This line displays the main menu names. You select a menu command to perform operations such as saving a file, formatting text, or printing a document. You select a menu command in Excel and PowerPoint the same way as you would in Word.

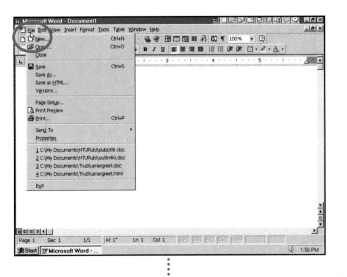

1 Point to **File** in the menu bar and click the left mouse button. This opens the File menu, which contains a list of File commands.

Missing Link

When you select a command followed by an ellipsis, Word displays a dialog box. Some dialog boxes have more than one set of options, indicated by tabs at the top of the dialog box. You can display a different set of options by clicking a tab.

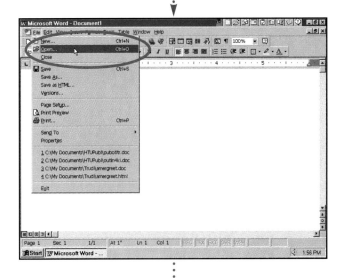

2 Point to **Open** and click the left mouse button. This selects the Open command, and Word opens the Open dialog box.

3 For now, click **Cancel** in the dialog box to close the box. ■

Puzzled?

To close a menu without making a selection, press the **Esc** key or click anywhere outside of the menu.

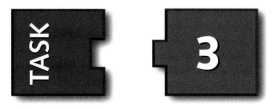

Using Shortcut Menus

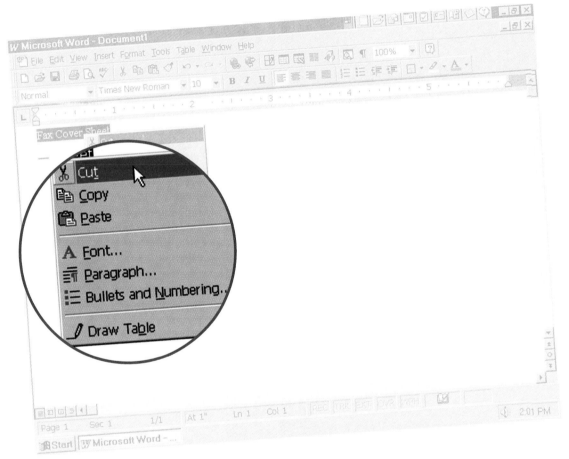

"Why would I do this?"

The shortcut menus include just those commands you need to use for the currently selected text, cell(s), or an object such as a chart. You might want to use a shortcut menu to quickly edit or format text or cells.

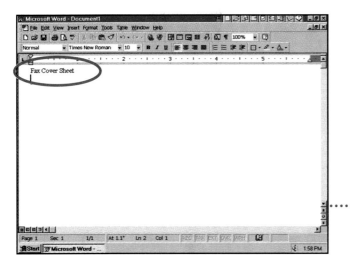

1 Type **Fax Cover Sheet** and press **Enter**. This enters text into the document. Then you can change that text using the short cut menu to see how the shortcut menu works.

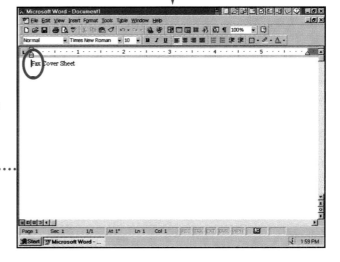

2 Click before the F in "Fax." This moves the insertion point to the place where you want to begin selecting text.

3 Hold down the left mouse button and drag the mouse across the words **Fax Cover Sheet**. Then release the left mouse button. This selects (or *highlights*) the text for which you want to open the shortcut menu.

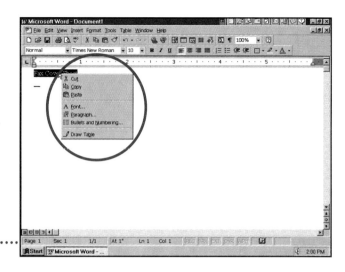

4 Point to the selected text and click the right mouse button. This opens a shortcut menu. In this menu, Word displays a list of commands for editing and formatting text.

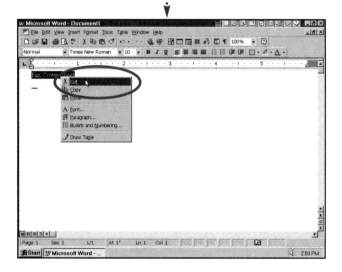

5 Click **Cut**. The Cut command moves the text from the document to the *Clipboard* (a temporary storage area). The selected text and the shortcut menu disappear. ■

Puzzled?

Sometimes you might display a shortcut menu that doesn't have the command you want to use. To leave a shortcut menu without making a selection, press the **Esc** key or click outside the menu.

TASK 4

Using the Toolbar

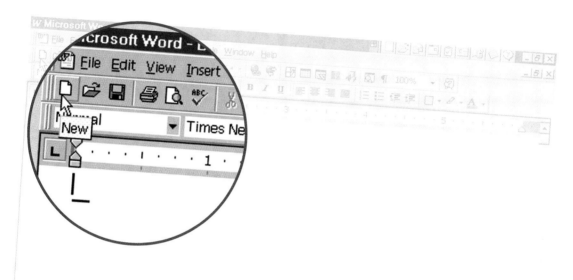

"Why would I do this?"

The Standard toolbar contains buttons for the most common commands you will use. The Formatting toolbar contains lists and buttons for the most common formatting commands you will use.

You need a mouse to use the toolbars. To perform a task, you select a toolbar button instead of a menu command (as a shortcut). If you're unsure what a toolbar button does, leave the mouse pointer on a toolbar button for a second or two. Word displays its name.

Task 4: Using the Toolbar

1 Point to the **New** button, the first button from the left on the Standard toolbar, and leave the mouse pointer on the button. Word displays the button's name (New) in a light yellow box near the button. This is the ScreenTip feature.

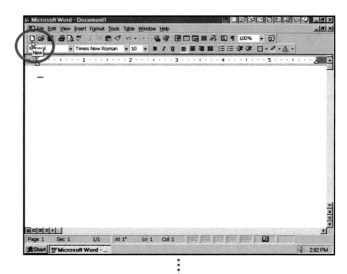

Puzzled?

If the ScreenTip does not appear right away, try moving the mouse pointer again and pause a few seconds.

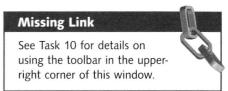

2 Click the **New** button. Word opens a new document and displays DOCUMENT2 in the title bar (this document is open on top of DOCUMENT1). Each time you create a new document, Word gives it a generic name until you save the document and give it a name of your own.

Missing Link

See Task 10 for details on using the toolbar in the upper-right corner of this window.

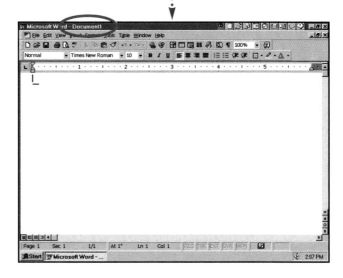

3 Click **File** in the menu bar, and then click **Close**. Word closes DOCUMENT2, and DOCUMENT1 becomes the active document again. ■

TASK 5

Getting Help

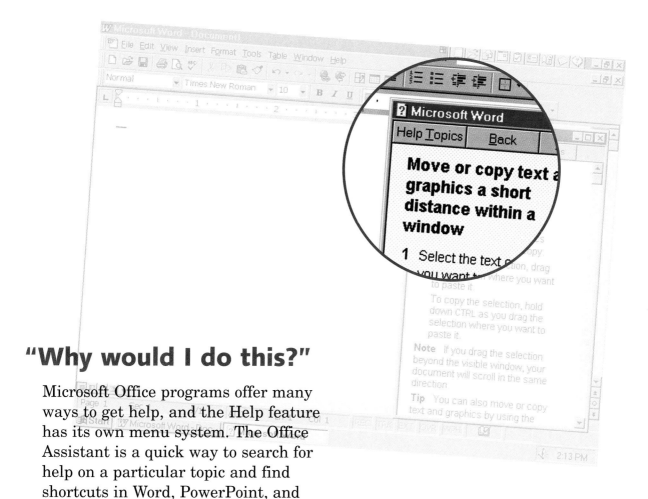

"Why would I do this?"

Microsoft Office programs offer many ways to get help, and the Help feature has its own menu system. The Office Assistant is a quick way to search for help on a particular topic and find shortcuts in Word, PowerPoint, and Excel.

First, let's use the Office Assistant to get help on how to copy text in Word. Then, you use the Office Assistant to learn about Word's many shortcuts.

Task 5: Getting Help

1 Click the **Office Assistant** button on the Standard toolbar, and Word opens the Office Assistant. You see the Office Assistant balloon, which allows you to search for help, get tips, and change options.

Missing Link

If the Office Assistant window is already open and the balloon isn't, click anywhere in the Office Assistant window (except on the yellow light bulb).

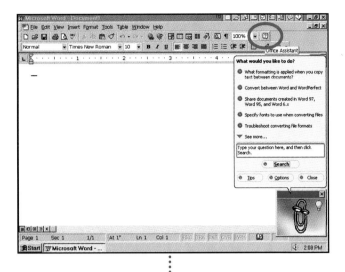

2 Type the topic you want help on, such as **copy text**, in the text box. This tells the Office Assistant what you would like to do.

Missing Link

You also can click the **?** (Help) button in the upper-right corner of any dialog box to get help on the command for which you are setting options.

3 Click the **Search** button. The Office Assistant displays a list of Help topics for copying text.

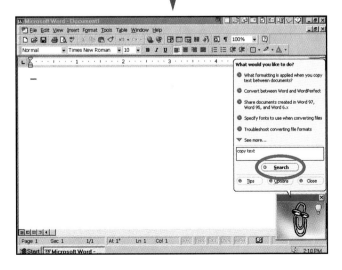

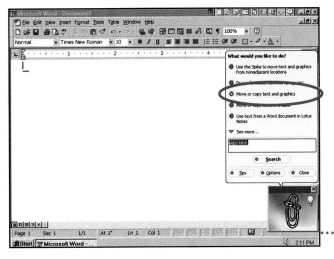

4 Point to the topic **Move or copy text and graphics** and click the left mouse button. This selects the Help topic. Word opens a dialog box, and you see a list of subtopics for copying text.

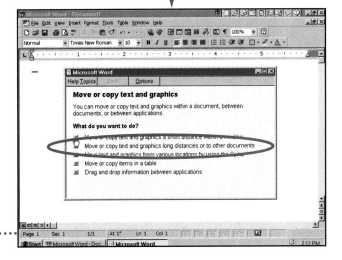

5 Point to the topic **Move or copy text and graphics a short distance within a window** and click the left mouse button. This selects the Help topic and opens a dialog box, which contains steps for you to follow in order to copy text.

6 Click the **Close** (X) button in the dialog box's title bar to close the dialog box.

7 Click the yellow light bulb in the Office Assistant window. The Office Assistant displays one of Word's shortcuts (which could be called "F.Y.I.," "Try This," or "Tip of the Day") in a light yellow balloon.

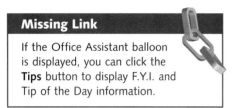

Missing Link

If the Office Assistant balloon is displayed, you can click the **Tips** button to display F.Y.I. and Tip of the Day information.

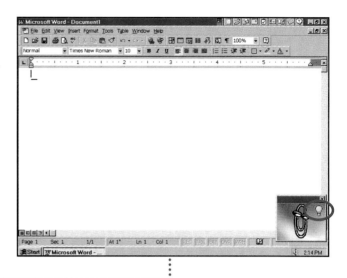

8 Click the **Back** or **Next** button, and the Office Assistant displays the previous tip (which could be an "F.Y.I.," a "Try This" or a "Tip of the Day").

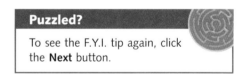

Puzzled?

To see the F.Y.I. tip again, click the **Next** button.

9 Click the **Close** button, and the Tips balloon disappears. Then click the **Close** (**X**) button in the Office Assistant window to close the Office Assistant. ■

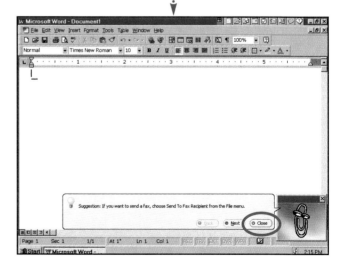

PART II

Managing Files

THIS PART GIVES YOU DETAILS about managing files in Word. However, keep in mind that these tasks also can be performed the same way in Excel and PowerPoint. You learn how to save your work and close a file, abandon a file, create a new file, open a file, and find a file. You also learn how to switch between Microsoft Office programs and cut and paste data between the applications.

By default, Word automatically saves your work every 10 minutes. You can change the time interval, or you can turn off the automatic save feature altogether. To make changes to the automatic save feature, choose **Tools**, **Options** and then click the **Save** tab. Type the number of minutes in the **Save AutoRecover Info** text box. To turn off automatic save, click to remove the X from the **Save AutoRecover Info** check box and click **OK**.

A document contains the work you do on-screen and is only in your computer's memory. When you save your document, the Microsoft Office program copies the information from memory to a file on disk (hard disk or floppy disk).

Saving a file that you previously saved is slightly different from saving a newly created file. When you save a file that was saved previously, you save the current version on-screen and overwrite the original version on disk. This means that you always have the most current version of your file stored on disk.

If you want to keep both versions—the on-screen version and the original—use the File Save As command to save the on-screen version with a different name. Saving a file with a new name gives you two copies of the same document, worksheet, or presentation with differences in their data. When you save a file with a new name, you also can save the file in a different directory or drive.

Saving a file does not remove it from the screen. To remove a file from the screen, you must close the file. Regardless of whether you've saved a file, you can close it using the File Close command.

When you open several files, they can overlap and hide files beneath other files. Word lets you rearrange the files so that some part of each file is visible. Arranging the open windows into smaller windows of similar sizes is handy when you want to copy or move text between two files that are side by side. You can use the Window Arrange All command to arrange the windows into smaller windows. If you want to display one file after you are finished using the window arrangement, close the files you do not want displayed. Then click the Maximize button in the document window you want to display. The file you want to display fills the screen.

Word's Find File feature lets you search for a file using any search criteria. For example, you can find a file using its file name, file type, text property, or last modified date as search criteria. When you choose the Open command, you can enter the search criteria in the Open dialog box, and Word quickly finds the file you want to use.

The Microsoft Office Shortcut Bar contains buttons for starting up and switching between Microsoft Office programs. The Microsoft Office button displays a list of Microsoft Office menu commands. These commands enable you to add and remove Microsoft Office programs, customize Microsoft Office, and get help.

After you learn how to use Word, Excel, PowerPoint, and Outlook, you can use Microsoft Office to share information between applications. For example, you can create a *hyperlink* to move between Office documents. A hyperlink is a pointer in a document that links to other documents. When you click a hyperlink, Office displays the document the link points to. A hyperlink appears as blue (default color) text in the document. This part shows you how to create a hyperlink to move from a Word document to an Excel worksheet.

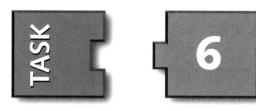

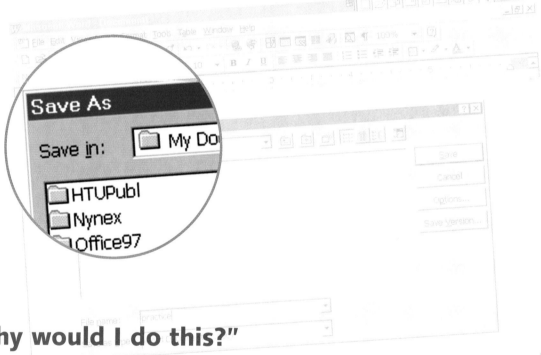

Saving and Closing a File

"Why would I do this?"

Until you save the file, your data is not stored on disk. Therefore, you can lose your data if something happens (such as a power loss). When you need the file again, you can retrieve it from the disk. You should save your work every 10 minutes and at the end of every work session. Then close the file if you want to clear the screen. (If you really want to, Word also lets you close a previously saved file without saving the changes.)

You're going to save the document you have been working on in the previous tasks. You can save a blank document at any time and then enter text into the file later. Name the document PRAC-TICE (Word automatically adds the file extension DOC to the file name). Then close the PRACTICE.DOC file.

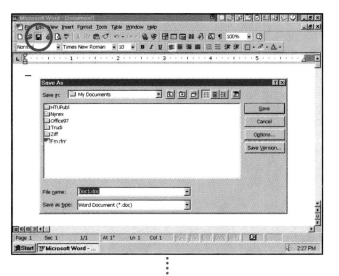

1 Click the **Save** button on the Standard toolbar. The first time you save the file, Word displays the Save As dialog box. This box lists the current folders and drive.

> **Missing Link**
>
> To save your files in a different folder, click the **Up One Level** button on the Save toolbar. In the **Save In** box, double-click the folder in which you want to save the file.

2 In the **File Name** text box, type **practice**. Word automatically adds the .DOC extension. Your file names can be as long as you want, and they can contain upper- or lowercase letters. Do not use spaces or punctuation.

> **Missing Link**
>
> To save the file with a different name, choose **File**, **Save As**. Enter a new name and location and click **Save**.

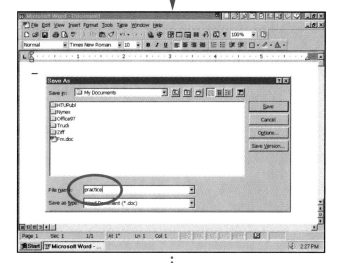

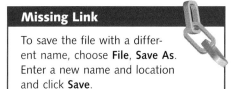

3 Click **Save** or press **Enter**. The file name, PRACTICE.DOC, appears in the title bar of the file.

> **Puzzled?**
>
> If you type a file name that already exists, Word asks Do you want to replace the existing file? If you do not want to replace that file, click **Cancel** and then type a new name.

4 Click the **Close** (X) button in the upper-right corner of the document window (on the right end of the menu bar) to close the file.

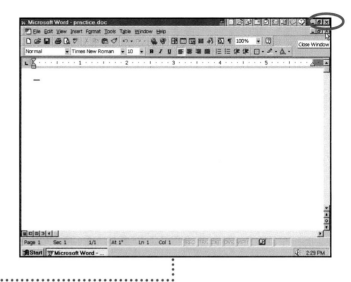

Missing Link

If you want to use this document in a version of Word for Windows earlier than Windows 95, limit the file name to no more than eight characters and a three-character file extension.

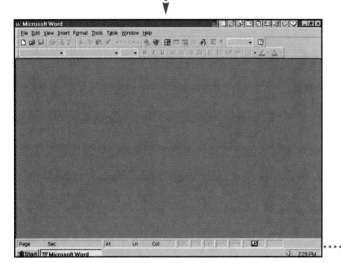

5 If you have not made changes, Word closes the active document. You then see just the menu bar, toolbars, and a blank window. From there, you can open a file, create a new document or template, or access Word Help.

6 If you have made changes, Word displays an alert box that reminds you to save the changes. Click **Yes** to save the changes and close the document. If you don't want to save the changes, click **No** to ignore them and close the document. ∎

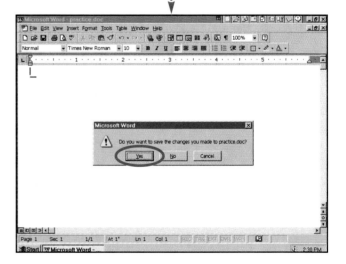

Puzzled?

If you decide that you still need to make changes, click **Cancel** in the alert box. Word takes you back to the document.

TASK

7

Creating a New File

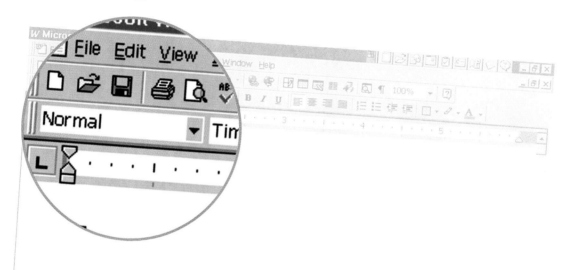

"Why would I do this?"

Word presents a new blank document each time you start the program. You can create another new document at any time. For example, when you have saved and closed one document, you might want to begin a new one.

In this task, you'll create a new blank document. For the purposes of this part, you'll then close that document without making any changes to it.

Task 7: Creating a New File

1 Click the **New** button in the Standard tool-bar. A blank document appears on-screen with the title DOCUMENT2 in the title bar. (This number increases by one for each document you create during a session.)

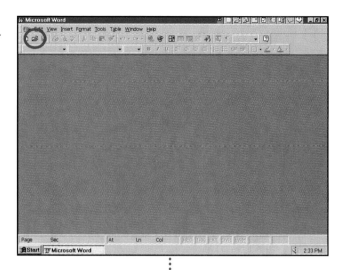

Missing Link

You also can click the **New Office Document** button on the Office Shortcut Bar and double-click the **Blank Document** icon to create a new blank document.

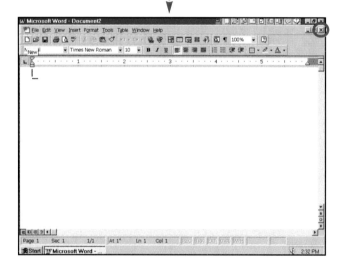

2 Click the **Close** (X) button in the upper-right corner of the document window to close the file. ■

Puzzled?

If you have more than one document open, you can switch among documents using the Window menu. Simply click **Window** in the menu bar, and then choose an open document from the list at the bottom of the menu.

Opening a File

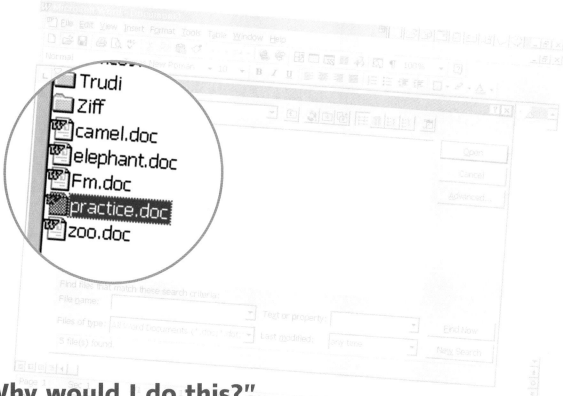

"Why would I do this?"

After you save a file, you can open it
again later to view it or make changes
to it. When you want to work with a file
again, use the Open button on the
Standard toolbar to open the closed document file. The maximum number of
files you can open at one time depends
on your system memory, but it's a good
idea to keep the number of open windows to a minimum.

Task 8: Opening a File

1 Click the **Open** button on the Standard toolbar. Word displays the Open dialog box. To see the date, time, or more information about the files, click the **Details** button on the Open toolbar.

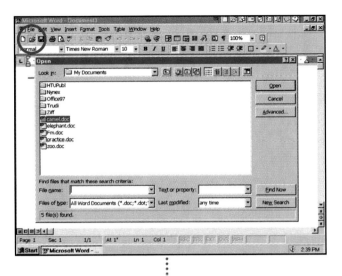

> **Missing Link**
>
> Alternatively, you can click the **Open Office Document** button on the Office Shortcut Bar, or you can open the **File** menu and choose one of the last four files you worked on.

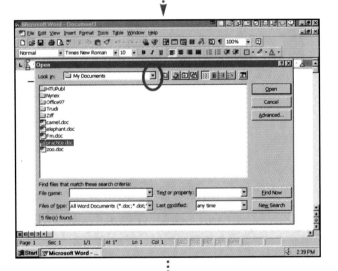

2 If necessary, click the **Look In** drop-down arrow and select the folder from the list. To move up a folder level, click the **Up One Level** button on the Open toolbar. If you double-click a subfolder, its contents appear in the files and folders list.

> **Missing Link**
>
> If you know the file name, you can type it in the **File Name** text box and click **Open**.

3 If necessary, click the down scroll arrow in the **File Name** list to find the PRAC-TICE.DOC file. When you find it, double-click **PRACTICE.DOC** to open that file. Word displays the file on-screen, as you can tell by the file name in the title bar. ∎

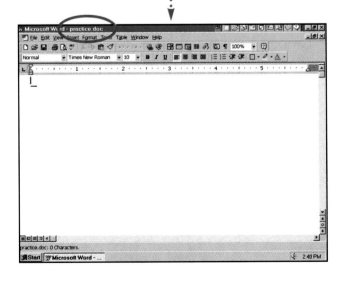

> **Puzzled?**
>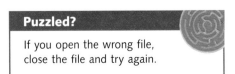
> If you open the wrong file, close the file and try again.

TASK

9

Finding a File

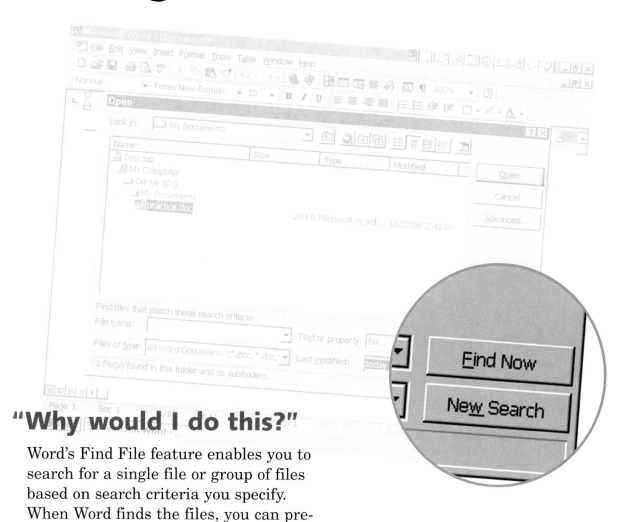

"Why would I do this?"

Word's Find File feature enables you to search for a single file or group of files based on search criteria you specify. When Word finds the files, you can preview and open the document you want. The Find File feature comes in handy when you can't remember the name of a file.

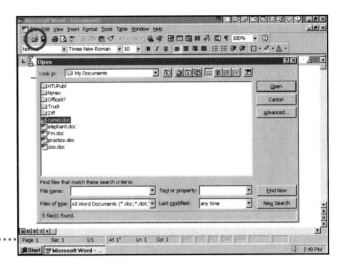

1 Click the **Open** button on the Standard toolbar. Word displays the Open dialog box.

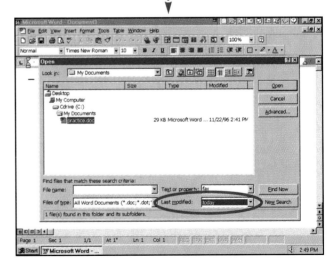

2 Type what you want to search for in the **Text or Property** text box at the bottom of the Open dialog box. For example, type **fax** to find any document that contains the word "fax."

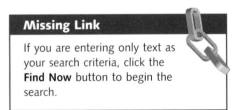

Missing Link

If you are entering only text as your search criteria, click the **Find Now** button to begin the search.

3 Click the **Last Modified** drop-down arrow and choose **Today** to specify that you want to find only documents you've worked with today. Word begins searching and highlights the document that matches the search criteria you specified.

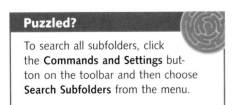

Puzzled?

To search all subfolders, click the **Commands and Settings** button on the toolbar and then choose **Search Subfolders** from the menu.

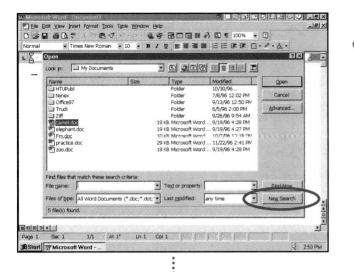

4 Click the **New Search** button in the Open dialog box to clear the current search criteria. You can then begin a new search if necessary.

> **Puzzled?**
>
> If Word doesn't find any files based on the specified search criteria, click the **New Search** button and try again using different criteria.

5 To close the Open dialog box, click the **Cancel** button. ■

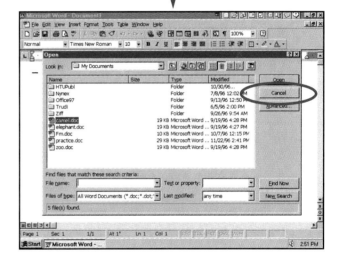

Switching Between
Microsoft Office Programs

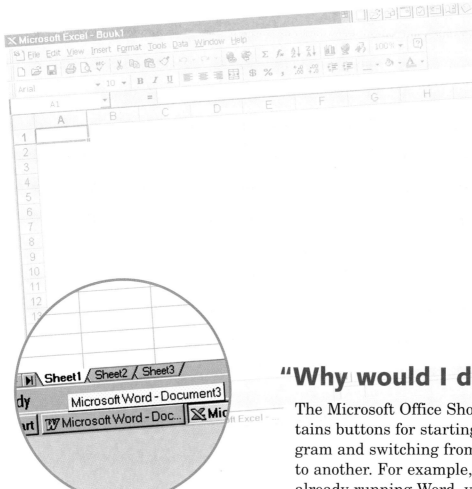

"Why would I do this?"

The Microsoft Office Shortcut Bar contains buttons for starting an Office program and switching from one program to another. For example, if you are already running Word, you can create a new Excel spreadsheet by clicking the **New Office Document** button on the Office Shortcut Bar instead of returning to the Windows Programs menu to start Excel.

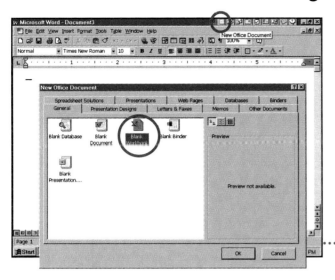

1 Click the **New Office Document** button on the Office Shortcut Bar. Word displays the New Office Document dialog box.

2 Double-click the **Blank Workbook** icon to start the Microsoft Excel program. The Microsoft Excel application window appears. At this point, you could do whatever work you needed to do in Excel.

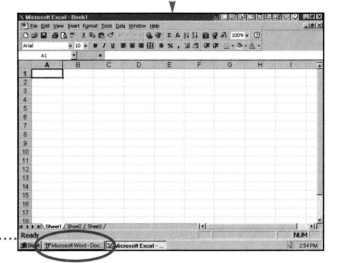

3 To switch back to the Word document, click the **Microsoft Word** button on the Windows taskbar.

Puzzled?

If you switch to the wrong program, just click the button on the Windows taskbar to switch to the correct program.

4 You're returned to the Word program, where you can continue working on your Word document. ▦

Missing Link

To have both application windows visible on-screen, you can tile the documents. Right-click anywhere in the Windows taskbar and choose **Tile Horizontally** or **Tile Vertically**.

TASK 11

Copying and Pasting Data Between Microsoft Office Programs

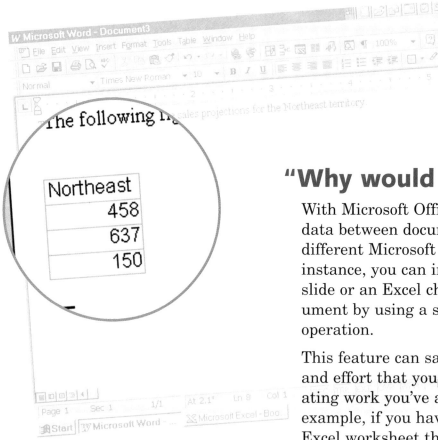

"Why would I do this?"

With Microsoft Office, you can share data between documents created with different Microsoft Office programs. For instance, you can insert a PowerPoint slide or an Excel chart into a Word document by using a simple cut and paste operation.

This feature can save you a lot of time and effort that you might spend recreating work you've already done. For example, if you have sales data in an Excel worksheet that you need to provide to your boss in a report, you can copy and paste it instead of retyping it (and running the risk of introducing new errors).

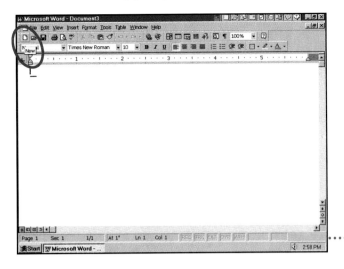

1 Click the **New** button on the Standard toolbar. This selects the File, New command. A blank document appears on-screen.

2 Type the text that appears in this figure so that your computer screen matches the one shown in the book.

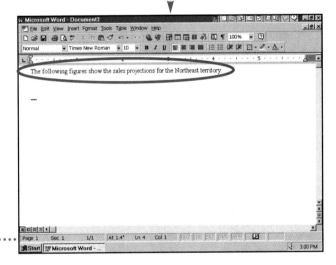

3 Click the **New Office Document** button on the Office Shortcut Bar and double-click the **Blank Workbook** icon (as you learned in Task 10). This opens the Excel program.

4 Click the **New** button on Excel's Standard toolbar to create a new worksheet. In cell A1, type **Northeast** and press **Enter**. Excel accepts the entry and moves down one cell. Then type **458** and press **Enter**; type **637** and press **Enter**; type **150** and press **Enter**. This enters data into the spreadsheet—the data that you want to copy and paste into the memo.

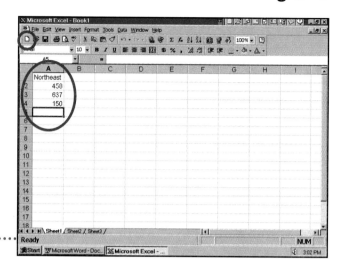

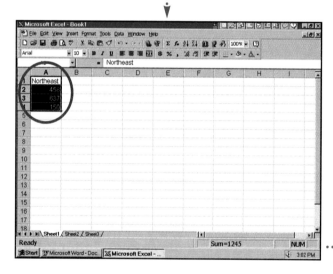

5 Click cell **A1**, which contains the word "Northeast." Then drag the mouse across cells **A2** through **A4** (the data you want to copy and paste into the memo). Excel highlights the data as you drag over it.

6 Click the **Copy** button on Excel's Standard toolbar. This places the data on the Clipboard. A marquee surrounds the data that you copied.

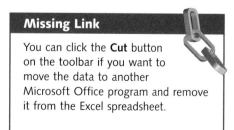

Missing Link

You can click the **Cut** button on the toolbar if you want to move the data to another Microsoft Office program and remove it from the Excel spreadsheet.

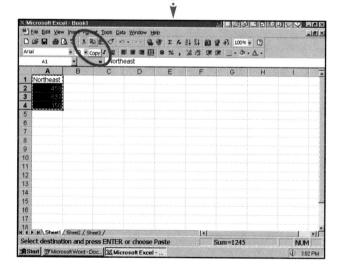

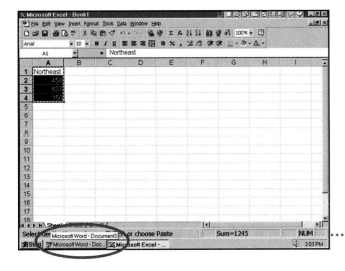

7 Click the **Microsoft Word** button on the Windows taskbar to switch to the Word program.

8 The insertion point currently appears at the end of the Word document. If that's where you want to paste the Excel data, click the **Paste Cells** button on the Word toolbar. Word pastes the worksheet data into the memo. (If you want to place the data elsewhere in the memo, move the insertion point before you click Paste Cells.) ▓

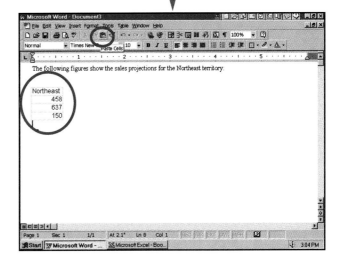

TASK 12

Creating Hyperlinks to Move Between Office Application Documents

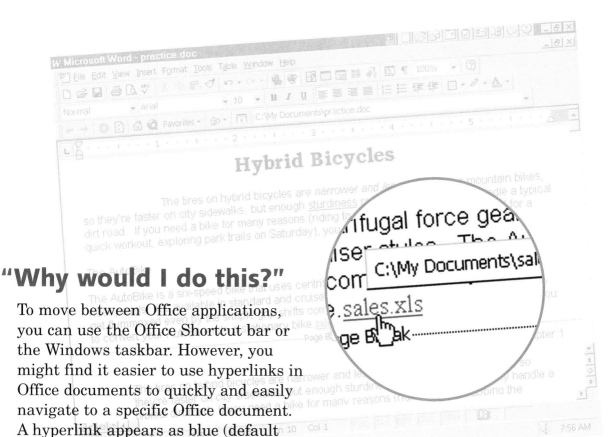

"Why would I do this?"

To move between Office applications, you can use the Office Shortcut bar or the Windows taskbar. However, you might find it easier to use hyperlinks in Office documents to quickly and easily navigate to a specific Office document. A hyperlink appears as blue (default color) text that you can click to move to a particular document. For instance, you may want to move from a report in Word to an Excel worksheet to further explain the report.

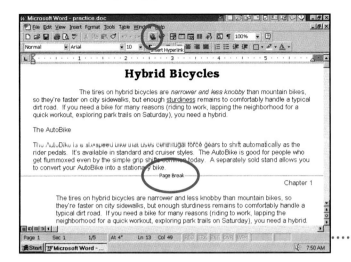

1 Start Word and open the **practice.doc** file. Click after the period in the last paragraph at the end of page 1 to place the insertion point where you want to insert a hyperlink. Then click the **Insert Hyperlink** button on the Standard toolbar. The Insert Hyperlink dialog box opens.

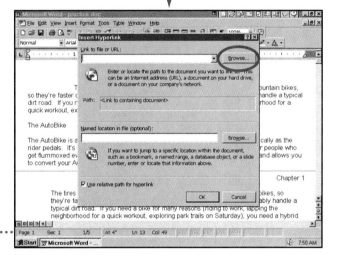

2 Click the **Browse** button, and the Link to File dialog box appears.

3 Select the file to which you want to set a link. For example, double-click **sales.xls**. Office returns you to the Insert Hyperlink dialog box and displays the document path name in the Link to File or URL text box.

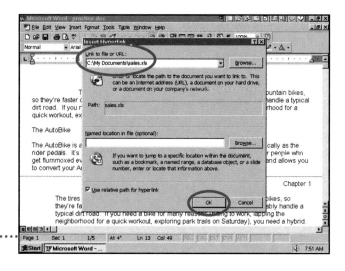

4 Click **OK** to confirm your choice. The hyperlink appears at the end of page 1; it contains the file name sales.xls in blue.

5 Point to the hyperlink. The mouse pointer changes to a hand pointer, and the ScreenTip that contains the document path name appears above the pointer. Click the hyperlink.

6 Excel opens and you see the sales.xls worksheet. Click the **Close** (X) button in the upper-right corner of the Excel window to close Excel. ■

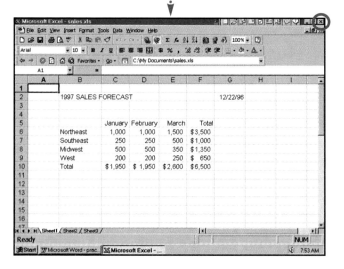

PART III

Entering and Editing Text in Word

▲ ● ■ ▲ ● ■ ▲ ●

A NYTIME YOU OPEN an existing document to continue work, you're adding to that document. You use simple editing features to add text to an existing document. These features include Insert mode, which enables you to add new text around existing text. And in case you want to replace existing text with new, there's a feature that enables you to type new text over the top of existing text. This part discusses both modes for adding text.

To add text to any document, you either type in new text or cut and paste text from another document. It is even possible to merge another text file with the current one (called inserting a file).

The Find command enables you to search for specific text, character formatting (such as bold, italic, and underline), and paragraph formatting (such as indents and spacing). And working in conjunction with the Find feature, Word's Replace feature lets you change a word or phrase, character formatting, paragraph formatting, or any special character throughout the document quickly and easily.

With the Spelling feature, you can use custom dictionaries for medical, legal, and technical documents to ensure accuracy when spell checking special terms for documents in those fields.

Sometimes a document is too large to be displayed on one screen at one time. To place text in other areas of the document, you must be able to move to the desired locations. There are many ways to move around the document. You can use the arrow keys to move one character and one line at a time, or you can use key combinations to quickly move around the document.

You can navigate around the document with the following arrow keys and key combinations:

To Move	Press
Right or left one character	→ or ←
Up or down one line	↑ or ↓
To the previous word or the next word	Ctrl+← or Ctrl+→
To the beginning of a line or the end of a line	Home or End
To the beginning of the document or the end of the document	Ctrl+Home or Ctrl+End
To the previous screen or the next screen	PgUp or PgDn

In this part, you also learn how to move quickly around the document with the mouse and how to use Word's Go To command to jump to a specific page that is out of view.

After you enter data, you can overwrite text and separate and combine paragraphs. This part shows you how to *select*, or highlight, text to define the portion of it that you want to overtype, delete, move, copy, edit, or enhance. Word highlights text you select.

You can select text with the following key combinations:

To Select	Press
One character to the right of the insertion point	Shift+→
One character to the left of the insertion point	Shift+←
One line above the insertion point	Shift+↑
One line below the insertion point	Shift+↓
From the insertion point to the end of the line	Shift+End
From the insertion point to the beginning of the line	Shift+Home

To deselect text using the keyboard, press any of the respective arrow keys.

In this part, you learn how to select text quickly with the mouse. You also learn how to delete text, copy text, move text to other locations in the document, and undo mistakes.

13

Adding and Overwriting Text

"Why would I do this?"

By default, Word is in Insert mode. In Insert mode, you type text at the insertion point, and existing text moves forward to make room for the new text. However, you might run into situations in which you want to enter new text *and* delete existing text. You can overwrite text, which replaces the existing text with new text as you type. This is handy when you want to correct typing errors.

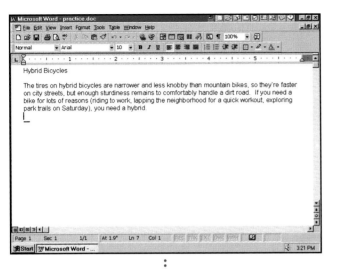

1 Open the **PRACTICE.DOC** file and type the text that appears in this figure. When you finish, your computer screen should match the screen shown here.

Puzzled?

If you make a mistake when typing text, use the Backspace key to delete characters to the left of the insertion point, or use the Delete key to delete characters to the right of the insertion point.

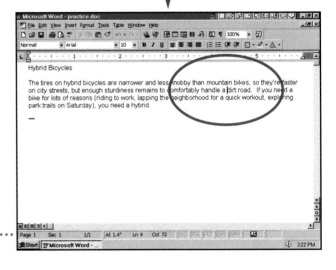

2 Place the insertion point in the location where you want to insert text. For example, click before the word "dirt." (You can place the insertion point by clicking the location or by using the arrow keys.)

3 Type **typical** and press the **Spacebar**. As you type, the new text appears, and existing text moves to the right.

4 Now suppose that you want to replace existing text with new text. Select the text you want to overwrite. For this example, click before the word "lots" and drag over to the word "reasons."

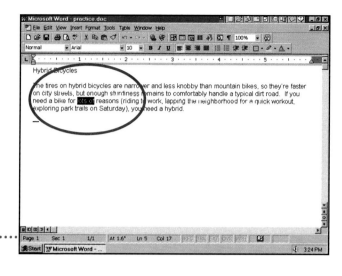

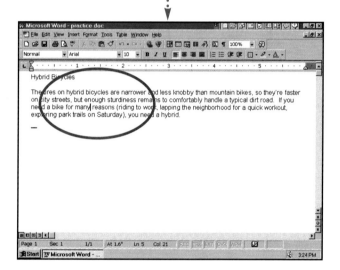

5 Type **many**, and the new text replaces all the selected text. ■

TASK 14

Moving Around the Document

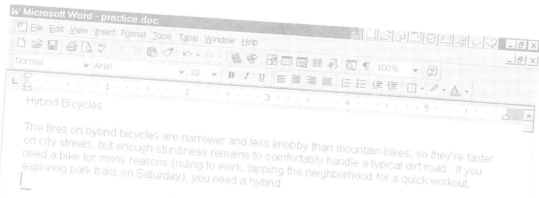

"Why would I do this?"

Because you typically make changes to your text in multiple areas of a document, you need shortcuts for moving around the document. Using a mouse is often the easiest way to move around the document; simply use the vertical and horizontal scroll bars to move to and view other portions of the document.

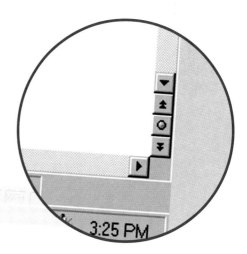

In addition, the Go To command on the Edit menu is useful for jumping to any page that is out of view in the current document. Perhaps you're working on page 4, and you want to make a change on page 1. You can get there quickly with the Go To command.

Task 14: Moving Around the Document

1 Click twice on the down scroll arrow at the bottom of the vertical scroll bar. Word moves down through the document one or more lines at a time, depending on the length of the document.

Missing Link

You can point to the up, down, left, or right scroll arrow and hold down the mouse button to scroll the document continuously in a particular direction.

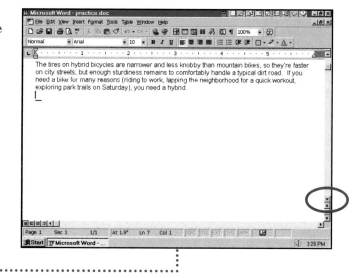

2 Click twice on the up scroll arrow at the top of the vertical scroll bar. Word scrolls up through the document one or more lines at a time, depending on the length of the document.

Missing Link

You can click the **Previous Find/Go To** double up arrow button at the bottom of the vertical scroll bar to move to the previous page. Click the **Next Find/Go To** double down arrow button at the bottom of the vertical scroll bar to move to the next page.

3 Click somewhere in the middle of the vertical scroll bar, and Word moves the document one window length at a time in that direction. Notice that the scroll box is at the bottom of the vertical scroll bar.

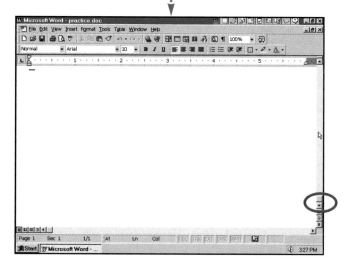

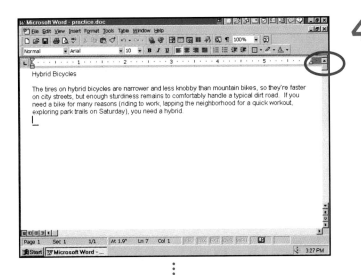

4 Click on and drag the scroll box to the top of the vertical scroll bar. This moves through the document quickly in the direction of the scroll box. In this case, Word moves up and displays the beginning of the document.

Puzzled?

If you run out of room to move the mouse on your desktop or mouse pad, just lift the mouse and then put it down in the middle of the mouse pad.

5 Click on and drag the scroll box to the far right of the horizontal scroll bar. Word moves quickly through the document in the direction of the scroll box.

Missing Link

Scrolling through the document doesn't move the insertion point; it remains in its current position until you click within the document window. To move the insertion point, scroll to and then click in the position where you want the insertion point to appear.

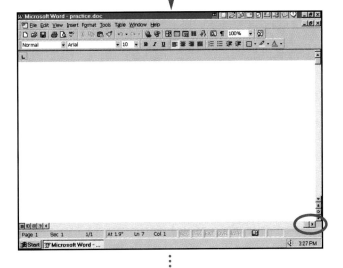

6 Scroll to the bottom of the document, and then press **Ctrl+Enter** to insert a page break. Word moves the insertion point to page 2. You see a dotted line and the words Page Break. (Be sure Word is in Normal view. Use Page Layout view to see the new blank page, as discussed in Part 5, "Viewing and Printing the Word Document.")

61

7 Press **F5** (the Go To key), and Word opens the Find and Replace dialog box. As you can see in this figure, the Go To tab is currently selected, and the insertion point is in the Enter Page Number text box.

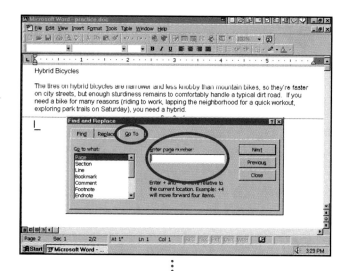

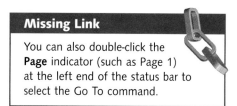

Missing Link

You can also double-click the **Page** indicator (such as Page 1) at the left end of the status bar to select the Go To command.

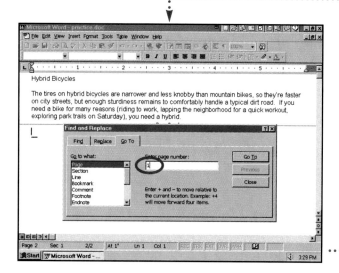

8 In the **Enter Page Number** text box, enter the number of the page you want to go to. For this example, type **1**.

9 Press **Enter**, and page 1 becomes the current page. Click the **Close** button to close the Go To dialog box. ■

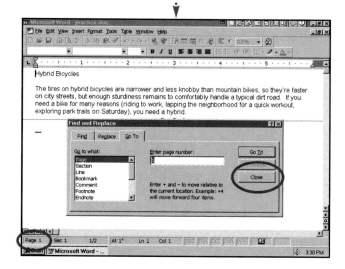

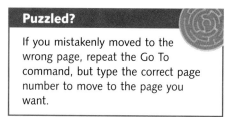

Puzzled?

If you mistakenly moved to the wrong page, repeat the Go To command, but type the correct page number to move to the page you want.

Separating and Combining Paragraphs

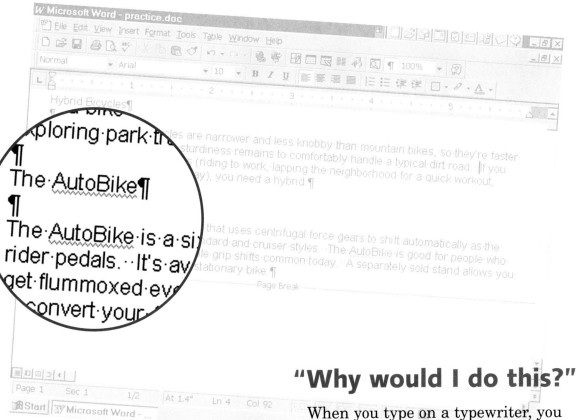

"Why would I do this?"

When you type on a typewriter, you have to press Enter at the end of each line. However, that's not true in Word. In Word, when text reaches the end of the line, Word automatically wraps the text to the next line. You press Enter only when you want to enter a hard return at the end of a short line, to place a blank line between paragraphs, or to end a paragraph.

1 Place the insertion point where you want to insert a blank line. For example, click at the end of the first sentence. (Be sure to click after the period.)

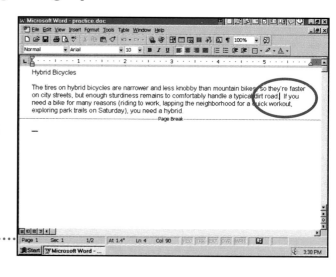

2 Press **Enter** to end the current paragraph and start a new one. Word inserts a paragraph mark in the document.

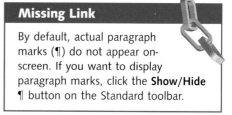

Missing Link

By default, actual paragraph marks (¶) do not appear on-screen. If you want to display paragraph marks, click the **Show/Hide** ¶ button on the Standard toolbar.

3 Press **Enter** again to start another line. The first two lines of text are now separated by a blank line. (You can press **Delete** twice to delete the two blank lines.)

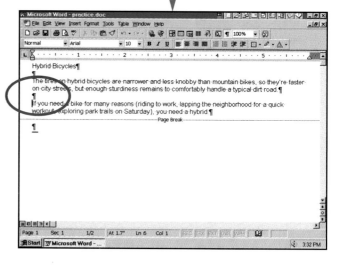

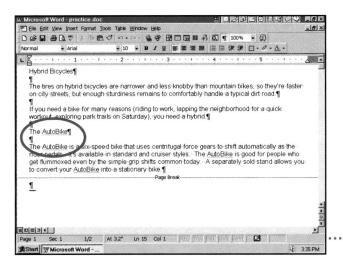

4 Click at the beginning of the blank line below the second paragraph. Press **Enter** to insert a blank line. Then type the new heading and paragraph that appear in this figure.

5 Click at the end of the second paragraph (after the period) and press **Delete**. Word deletes the paragraph mark at the end of the current paragraph, and all of the text after that moves up to fill the space.

Puzzled?

To split the paragraphs and add a blank line between them, place the insertion point where you want the break to appear. Then press **Enter** two times.

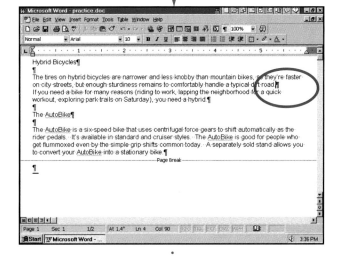

6 Press **Delete** again to delete the blank line between the paragraphs. The third paragraph moves up to become part of the second paragraph. Then press the **Spacebar** twice to insert two spaces between the two sentences. ■

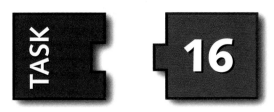

Selecting Text

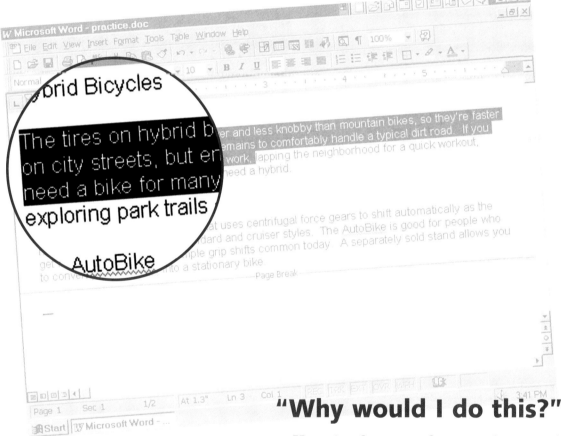

"Why would I do this?"

Knowing how to select text is essential because most of the commands and options in Word operate on selected text. For example, you may want to select a title so that you can issue the command to make it bold or larger. You can select any block of text—a word, line, sentence, or paragraph.

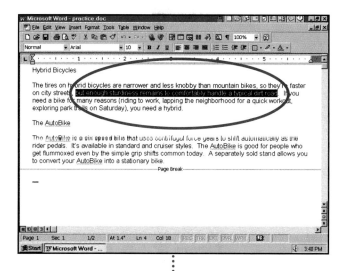

1 Place the mouse pointer at the beginning of the text you want to select, press and hold down the left mouse button, and drag the mouse pointer across the text you want to select. Word highlights the amount of text you specify.

Puzzled?

If you selected the wrong text, simply click anywhere else in the document. Then start over.

2 Double-click anywhere in the word *mountain* to select only that word.

Puzzled?

If you double-click a word to select it, and then you click (and hold) for the drag operation too quickly, the entire paragraph will be unintentionally selected. To avoid this, pause briefly before you click-and-hold to drag a word.

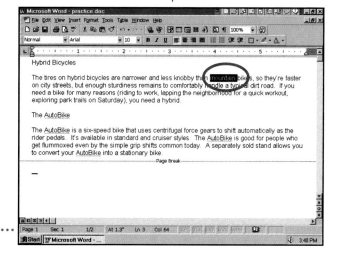

3 Position the mouse pointer in the left margin. When the pointer turns into a right-pointing arrow, click to select the line of text next to it. If you want to select more than one line, drag the mouse downward in the left margin.

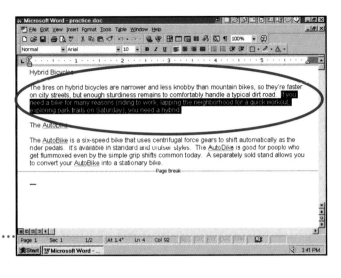

4 Hold down **Ctrl** and click anywhere within a sentence to select the entire sentence.

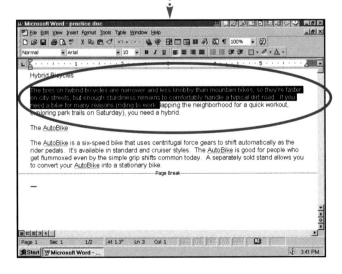

5 Position the mouse pointer in the left margin again. This time, when the pointer turns into a right-pointing arrow, double-click to select the whole paragraph next to it.

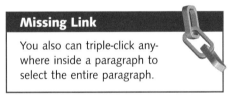

Missing Link

You also can triple-click anywhere inside a paragraph to select the entire paragraph.

6 Position the mouse pointer at the beginning of the text you want to select and click the left mouse button. Then press and hold down **Shift**, and click the end of the block of text. ■

Deleting Text and Using Undo

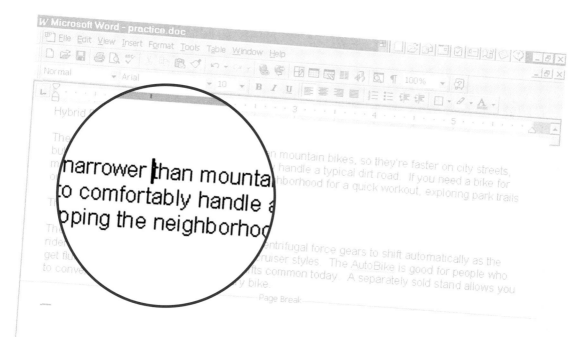

"Why would I do this?"

Sometimes you may find that text you initially typed into the document is incorrect and needs to be changed. Instead of overwriting the text to remove the entry, you can select any amount of text and then press the Delete key. To delete just one character, press the Delete key to delete characters to the right of the insertion point, or press Backspace to delete characters to the left.

If you accidentally delete the wrong text, you can use the Undo feature to restore it. You can also use the Undo feature to reverse many other types of actions: you can take out added text or remove character formatting, for example. And just in case you change your mind again, Word provides the Redo button. You can click Redo (the button that contains an arrow that curves to the right and down) on the Standard toolbar to "undo" an action you just reversed with Undo.

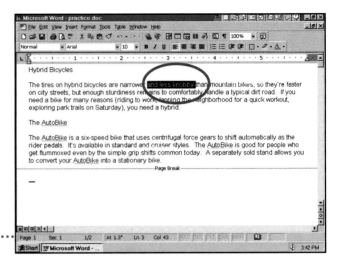

1 First highlight the text you want to delete. For this example, click before the word "and" in the first sentence of the first paragraph. Then drag across the words "and less knobby" to select all three words.

2 Press **Delete**. Word deletes the selected text, and the remaining text moves up (or over) to fill in the gap.

3 Click the **Undo** button on the Standard toolbar, and Word restores the deleted text. Click outside the selected text to deselect the text. ■

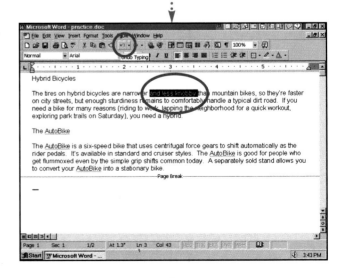

Missing Link

You can undo multiple actions by clicking the **Undo** drop-down arrow on the toolbar. You'll see a list of your actions, in order from the most recent to the least recent. (You can undo them in this order only.) Select the action(s) you want to undo, and Word reverses your action(s).

Copying Text

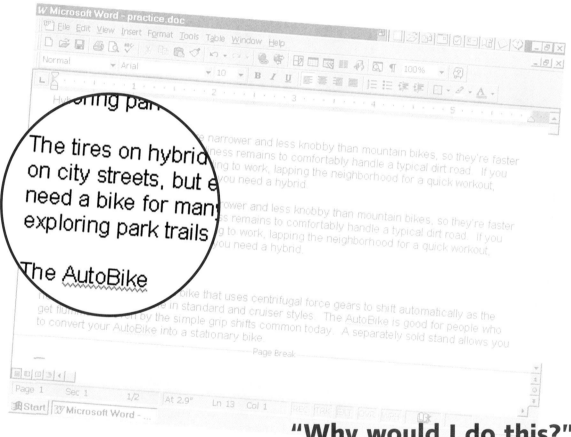

"Why would I do this?"

You can save the time of retyping information in the document by copying text over and over again. For example, you might want to copy a paragraph from one page to another page. That way you wouldn't have to type the paragraph over again, which saves you time and keystrokes.

1 Select the text you want to copy. In this case, triple-click in the first paragraph of your practice document. Word highlights the paragraph.

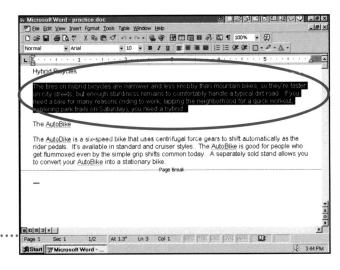

2 Click the **Copy** button on the Standard toolbar to copy the text to the Clipboard. The Clipboard is a temporary holding area for text and graphics.

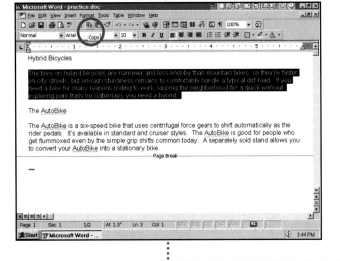

Missing Link

To copy text using the drag-and-drop method, select the text, press and hold the **Ctrl** key, and click the mouse button. A plus sign appears in a small box below the mouse pointer. Drag the text to the new location, and release the Ctrl key and the mouse button.

3 Next, place the insertion point where you want the copied text to appear. For example, click before the heading "The AutoBike."

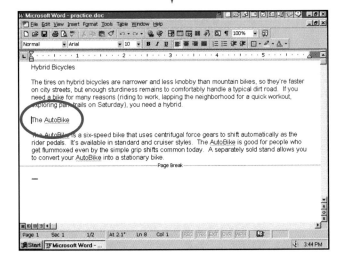

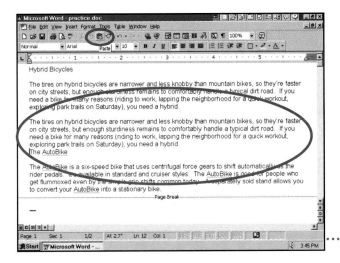

4 Click the **Paste** button on the Standard toolbar, and Word pastes the text from the Clipboard. The copied text now appears in the new location (as well as in the original location).

5 Press **Enter** to insert a blank line before the heading again. ■

Puzzled?

If you copied the wrong text or copied the data to the wrong location, click the **Undo** button on the Standard toolbar to undo the most recent copy. Or you can just delete the copied text and start over.

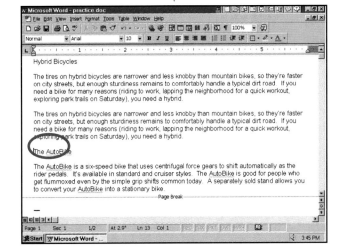

Moving Text

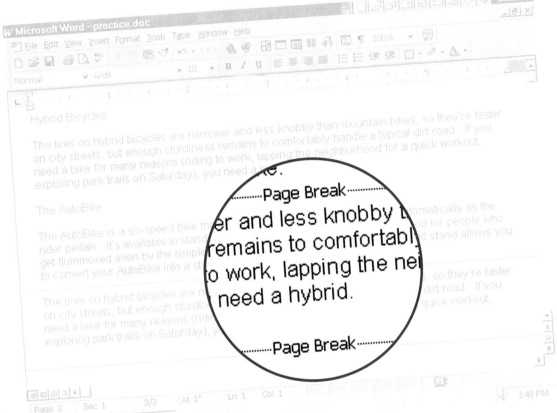

"Why would I do this?"

The Move command lets you move information from one location to another in the document. For example, you might want to swap the order of paragraphs, or you might want to move text in a document because the layout of the document has changed. By using the Move command instead of the Copy command, you don't have to go to the new location, enter the same text, and then erase the text from the old location.

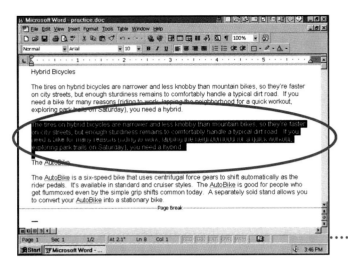

1 Click in the left margin next to the second paragraph and drag down to the blank line below the paragraph. This selects the text you want to move.

2 Click the **Cut** button on the Standard toolbar. Word cuts the text from the document and places it on the Clipboard (a temporary holding area). As you can see, the text no longer appears in its original location.

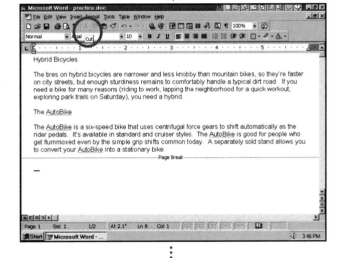

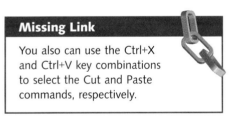

Missing Link

You also can use the Ctrl+X and Ctrl+V key combinations to select the Cut and Paste commands, respectively.

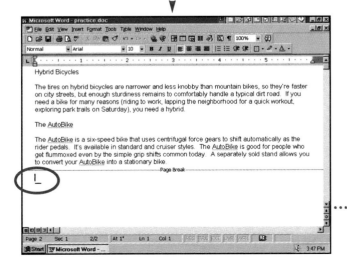

3 Place the insertion point where you want to move the text. For instance, click the blank line at the top of page 2.

4 Click the **Paste** button on the Standard toolbar to paste the text in the new location. The text now appears in the new location.

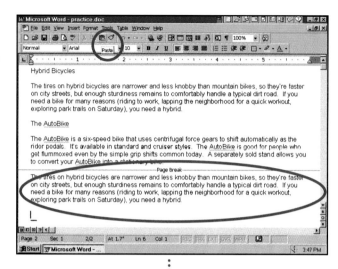

Missing Link

To use the drag-and-drop method for moving text, first select the text. Then move the mouse pointer back over the selected text, and click and hold the mouse button. A small box appears under the mouse pointer. Drag the text to the new location and release the mouse button.

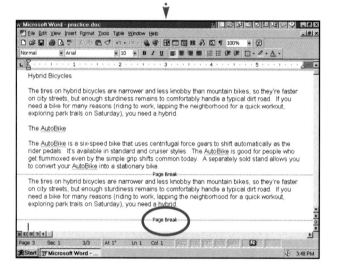

5 Press **Ctrl+Enter** to insert a page break. Word automatically inserts soft page breaks (a dotted line across the page) when the text reaches the bottom of a page. You can force a page break anywhere in a document with a hard page break (a dotted line across page with the words Page Break). To do so, press **Ctrl+Enter**. ■

Puzzled?

If you moved the wrong text or moved the text to the wrong location, click the **Undo** button on the Standard toolbar to undo the most recent move. Then start over.

TASK

20

Finding and Replacing Text

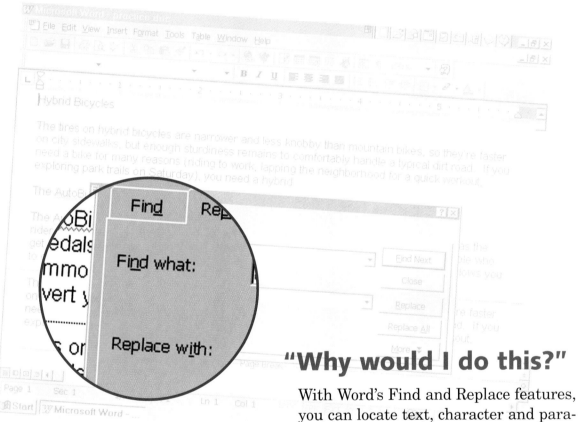

"Why would I do this?"

With Word's Find and Replace features, you can locate text, character and paragraph formatting or special characters and replace the original text or formatting with new. Suppose, for example, you have a word, phrase, formatting characteristic, or special character that you entered incorrectly throughout the document. You can use the Edit Replace command to have Word search for and replace all occurrences of the incorrect information with the correct information.

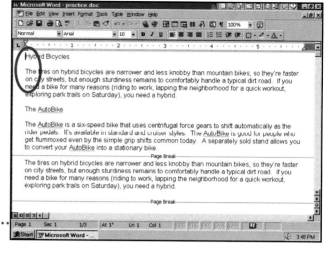

1 Press **Ctrl+Home** to move to the beginning of the document. When you begin the search, Word searches from the location of the insertion point forward. If you start the search in the middle of the document, Word searches the entire document—going from the middle to the end, and then to the beginning.

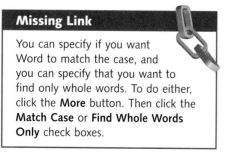

2 Press **Ctrl+F** to open the Find and Replace dialog box. The Find tab is currently selected, and the insertion point is in the Find What text box.

3 For this example, type **bike**. This text, called the *search string*, is what you want to find.

Missing Link

You can specify if you want Word to match the case, and you can specify that you want to find only whole words. To do either, click the **More** button. Then click the **Match Case** or **Find Whole Words Only** check boxes.

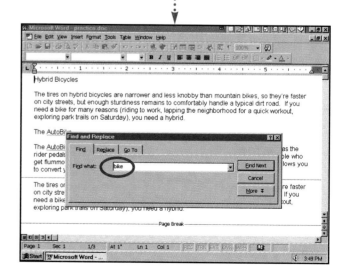

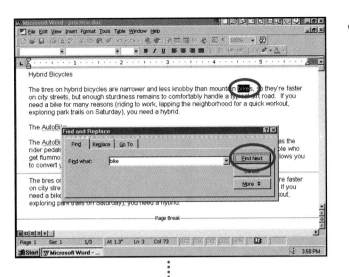

4 Click **Find Next** or press **Enter** to start the search. Word finds the first occurrence of the search string and highlights that text. The dialog box remains open on-screen. (If you can't see the text that Word finds, drag the Find dialog box by its title bar to uncover the selected text.)

Puzzled?

If Word does not find any matching text, you see an alert message. Click **OK** and try the search again, making sure you type the search string correctly.

5 Click **Find Next** to continue the search. Word finds the next occurrence of the search string and highlights that text. The dialog box remains open. Click **Cancel** to close the dialog box.

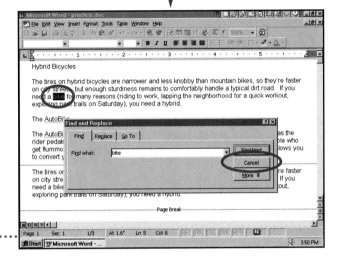

6 Before you start another search, press **Ctrl+Home** to move the insertion point to the beginning of the document. When you begin the search, Word searches from the location of the insertion point forward.

7 Press **Ctrl+H** to open the Find and Replace dialog box. The Replace tab is currently selected, and the insertion point is in the Find What text box. Notice that the previous search string appears in the Find What box.

Missing Link

The Replace dialog box also includes options that control how the program performs the search and replace operation.

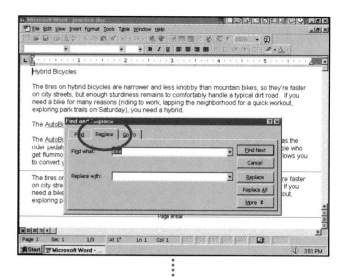

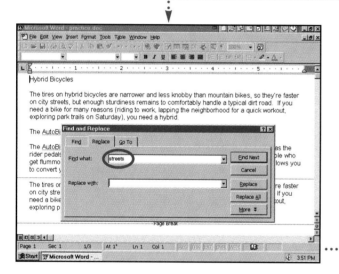

8 Enter a new search string if the one that's there is not correct. For this example, type **streets**. Press **Tab** to move the insertion point to the Replace With text box.

9 Type the text you want to use as the replacement. For example, type **sidewalks**.

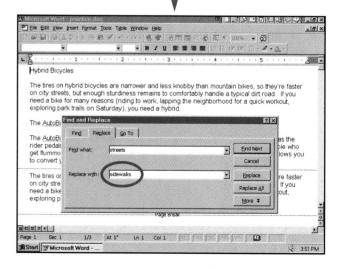

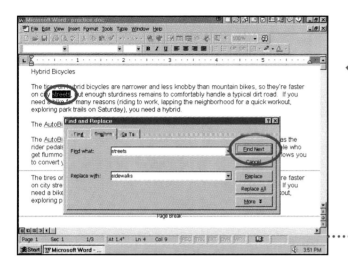

10 Click **Find Next** to start the search. Word finds the first occurrence of the search string and highlights that text. The dialog box remains open on-screen. (You can move the dialog box to see other text by dragging the dialog box's title bar.)

11 Click **Replace**. Word replaces the highlighted text with the replacement text and moves to the next occurrence of the search string. Click **Replace** for each occurrence that you want to replace. If you come to one you don't want to replace, click **Find Next** to skip it.

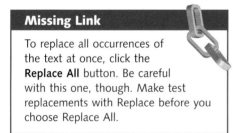

Missing Link

To replace all occurrences of the text at once, click the **Replace All** button. Be careful with this one, though. Make test replacements with Replace before you choose Replace All.

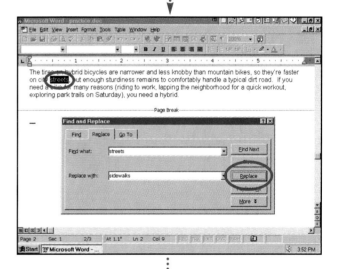

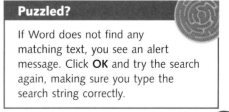

12 When Word finds no more occurrences of the search string, it displays an alert box. Click **OK** to close the alert box. Then click **Close** to close the dialog box. Now you can see the replaced text. ■

Puzzled?

If Word does not find any matching text, you see an alert message. Click **OK** and try the search again, making sure you type the search string correctly.

Checking Your Spelling

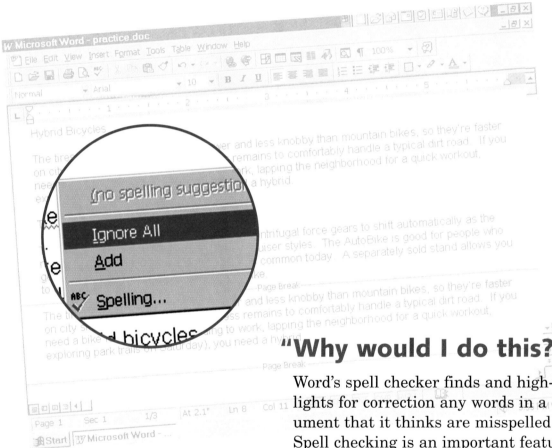

"Why would I do this?"

Word's spell checker finds and highlights for correction any words in a document that it thinks are misspelled. Spell checking is an important feature you should use to ensure that your documents look professional and letter perfect.

In addition, Word's AutoCorrect spell checker finds misspelled words automatically as you type them. Keep it turned on to prevent misspellings to begin with.

1 On page 1 of the practice document in the first sentence, remove the first occurrence of the letter *b* in the word "knobby." Click anywhere in the paragraph, and a wavy red line appears beneath the word to indicate that it contains a spelling error.

Missing Link

To use Word's spelling checker, press **F7** or click the **Spelling and Grammar** button on the Standard toolbar.

2 Move the mouse pointer to the first wavy red-underlined word and click the right mouse button. The Spelling shortcut menu appears. Choose a word from the suggested spelling list to change the word in the document.

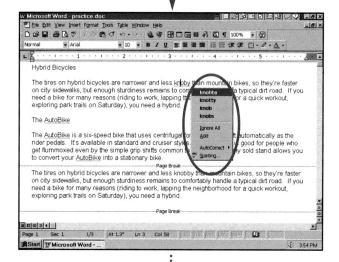

3 Right-click the next wavy red-underlined word. The Spelling shortcut menu appears. Choose **Ignore All** to remove the underline and tell Word to ignore all occurrences of this word (that is, not to stop on this word again). ■

Puzzled?

You can click **Add** to add any questionable word to the dictionary.

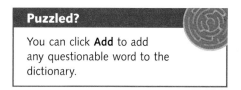

83

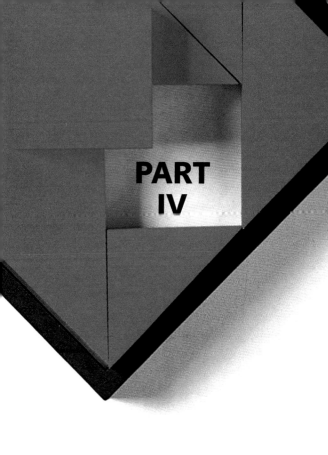

PART IV

Formatting Text in Word

FORMATTING THE DOCUMENT means that you can change the appearance of text in your document. With Word formatting tools, you can make your document more attractive and readable. In this part, you learn how easy it is to bold, italicize, and underline text; change the font; and change the font size. You also learn how to center and right-align text as well as indent text.

Making text bold and adding italics are among the most common formatting changes you make in a document. Similarly, you can underline text in your document using the Underline command. To underline text, you can use the Format Font command and then choose from several underline styles in the Font dialog box. The Underline styles include single, words only, double, and dotted. In this part, you learn how to apply the underline styles using the mouse.

A *font* is a style of type in a particular typeface and size. Word displays various fonts and font sizes in the Formatting toolbar. You can use the fonts provided by Word, as well as fonts designed especially for your printer. If Word does not have a screen version of the printer font you select, it substitutes a font. In such cases, the printout looks different from what you see on-screen.

You can apply fonts to a single word or any amount of text you want to change. You also can change the font size and font colors. The Font Color options in the Font dialog box let you change font colors easily. Many font colors are available in various shades, hues, and patterns that you can use to make your document more attractive. You can display text colors on a color monitor even if you print the document on a black and white printer. However, if you have a color printer, you'll benefit more from changing font colors.

You can align text left, center, right, or justified. The default alignment is Left. *Left alignment* means that text is aligned flush with the left margin. Center alignment centers text between the left and right margins. Right-aligned text appears flush with the right margin. Justified text spreads text between the left and right margins by expanding or contracting the spaces between words as necessary.

Left-aligned text has a "ragged right" edge on the page or column. Because it is a warm and readable format, left-alignment is usually used for conventional and office correspondence. Justified text, which has an orderly look, is generally used in multiple-column newsletters, newspapers, and magazines. In this part, you learn how to center and right-align text. If you want to justify text, you simply select the text you want to justify and click the **Justify** button on the Formatting toolbar.

Word provides another way to align paragraphs. You can indent paragraphs from the left margin, the right margin, or both margins. You can also indent only the first line of the paragraph.

In this part, you also learn how to create a bulleted list and a numbered list, set tabs and margins, number pages, and create headers and footers. And finally, you learn how to insert graphics to spice up your document and how to move and resize those graphics.

In essence, this part teaches you some of the most important formatting operations you need for enhancing the appearance and layout of your documents.

Making Text Bold, Italic, and Underlined

"Why would I do this?"

To draw attention to important text in a document, you can make the text bold, italic, and underlined—or a combination of them. For example, you may want to make the title of a book italic, or you might need to make the word "don't" bold in a letter to your kids.

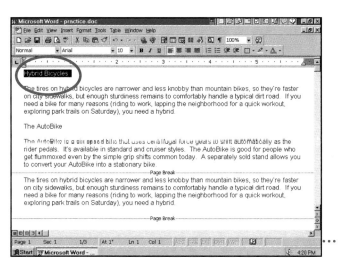

1 Open PRACTICE.DOC, or take a minute to enter the paragraphs shown in this figure. Then click in the left margin next to the title **Hybrid Bicycles**. This selects the text you want to make bold.

2 Click the **Bold** button on the Formatting toolbar, and Word applies bold to the selected text—in this case, the title.

Missing Link

You also can press **Ctrl+B** to select the Bold command. To remove the bold font style, select the bold text and press **Ctrl+B** again.

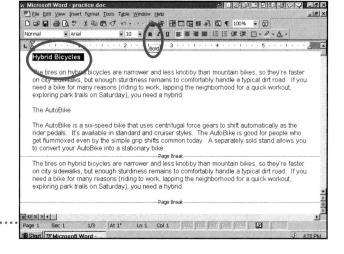

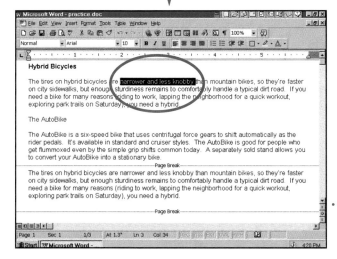

3 Next, select the text you want to italicize. Click anywhere on the word **narrower** and drag to the beginning of the word **than**.

4 Click the **Italic** button on the Formatting toolbar, and Word italicizes the selected text—in this case, the words "narrower and less knobby."

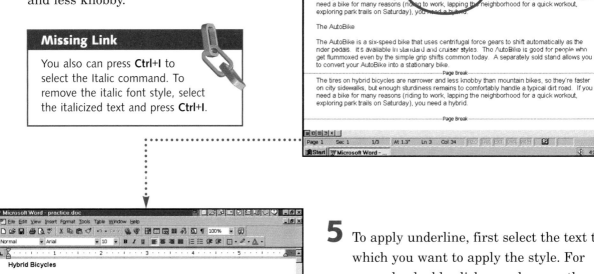

Missing Link

You also can press **Ctrl+I** to select the Italic command. To remove the italic font style, select the italicized text and press **Ctrl+I**.

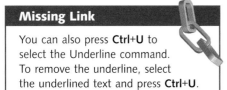

5 To apply underline, first select the text to which you want to apply the style. For example, double-click anywhere on the word **sturdiness**.

Puzzled?

To undo bold, italic, or underline font styles you've just applied, immediately click the **Undo** button on the Standard toolbar.

6 Click the **Underline** button on the Formatting toolbar, and Word underlines the text—in this case, "sturdiness." Click outside the selected text to deselect the text. ■

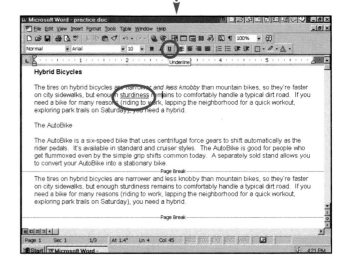

Missing Link

You can also press **Ctrl+U** to select the Underline command. To remove the underline, select the underlined text and press **Ctrl+U**.

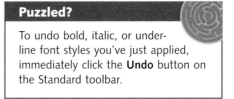

Changing the Font and Font Size

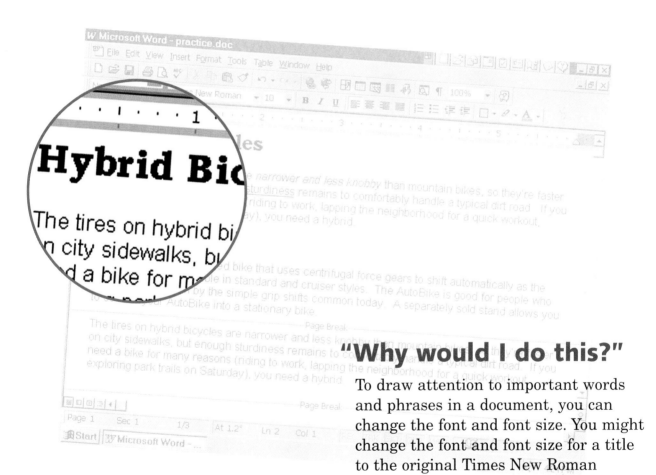

"Why would I do this?"

To draw attention to important words and phrases in a document, you can change the font and font size. You might change the font and font size for a title to the original Times New Roman 24-point, for example, to enhance the text and make the title stand out at the top of the document.

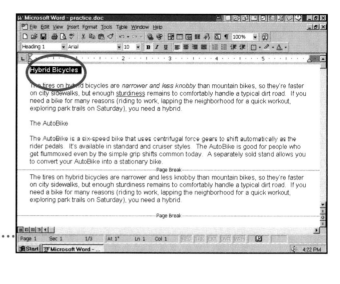

1 Select the text that you want to change. For example, click in the left margin next to the title **Hybrid Bicycles**.

2 Click the **Font** drop-down arrow on the Formatting toolbar. Word displays a list of available fonts.

3 Click any font in the list, such as **Bookman Old Style**, and Word changes the font of the selected text.

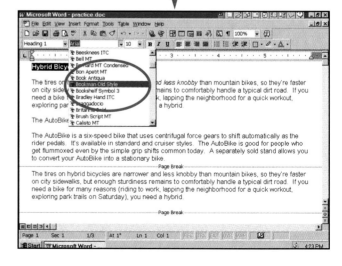

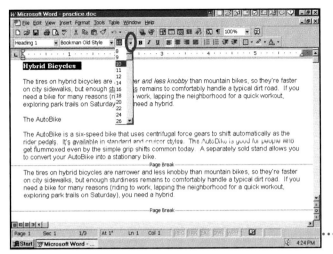

4 To change the size of the type, click the **Font Size** drop-down arrow on the Formatting toolbar. This displays a list of possible font sizes.

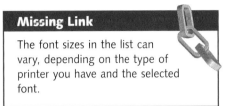

Missing Link

The font sizes in the list can vary, depending on the type of printer you have and the selected font.

5 Click a larger font size (a higher number), such as **18**, and Word changes the font size for the selected text. (If you know the font size you want, you can just type the number in the **Font Size** text box.)

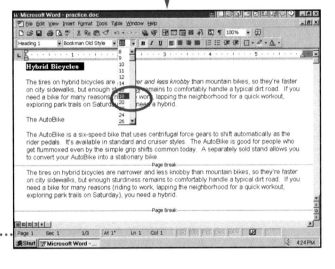

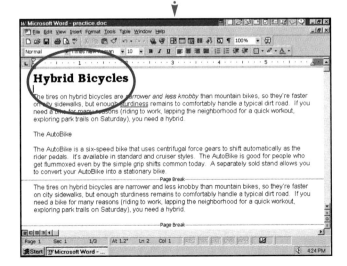

6 Click outside the selected text to deselect it. As you can see here, Word increases the text size according to your change. ■

Puzzled?

To undo a font change you just made, immediately click the **Undo** button on the Standard toolbar.

Centering and Right-Aligning Text

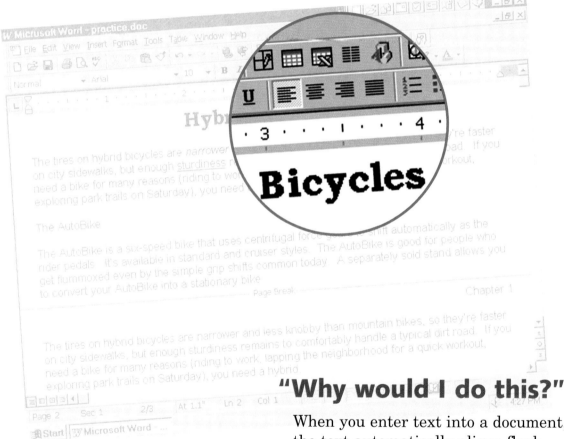

"Why would I do this?"

When you enter text into a document, the text automatically aligns flush (even) with the left margin. However, you can change the alignment of text at any time. You can make it centered, flush right, or justified (flush with both margins).

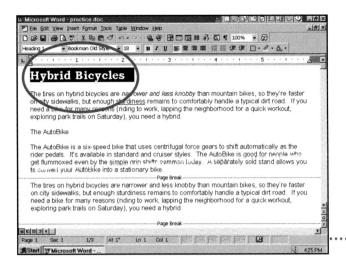

1 Click in the left margin next to **Hybrid Bicycles** to select the line of text you want to center.

2 Click the **Center** button on the Formatting toolbar, and Word centers the selected text—in this case, the chapter title.

Puzzled?

To undo your most recent alignment change, click the **Undo** button on the Standard toolbar.

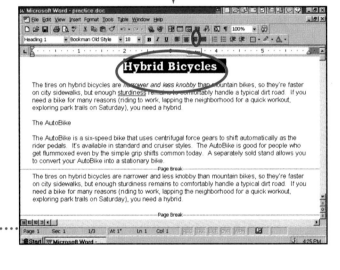

3 At the top of page 2, click to the left of the *T* in the word "The." Then type **Chapter 1** and press **Enter** twice.

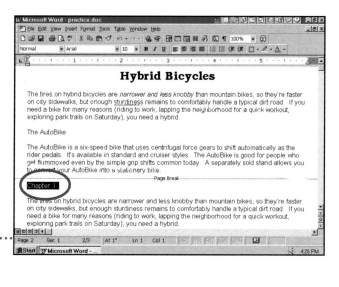

4 To right-align text, first select the text for which you want to change the alignment. For this example, click in the left margin next to **Chapter 1**.

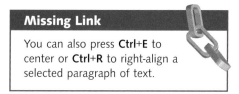

5 Click the **Align Right** button on the Formatting toolbar, and Word right-aligns the selected text (the title).

> **Missing Link**
>
> You can also press **Ctrl+E** to center or **Ctrl+R** to right-align a selected paragraph of text.

6 Click outside the selected text to deselect it. ■

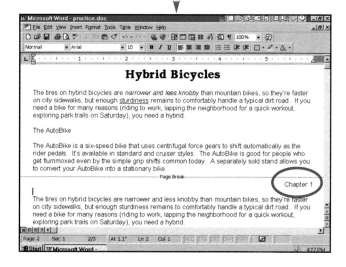

Indenting Text

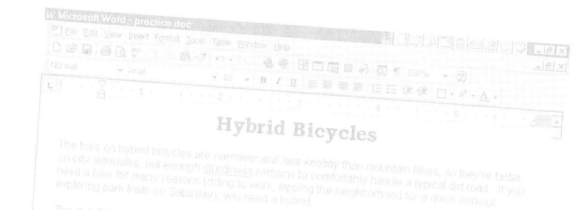

"Why would I do this?"

You can indent an entire paragraph to the right of the left margin to make it stand out. For example, if you were creating a contract, you might want to indent certain paragraphs to make them subordinate to other text. After you create the indent, you can adjust it by entering specific measurements or by using the Ruler.

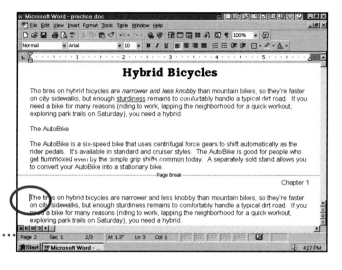

1 At the beginning of the paragraph on page 2, click before the *T* in the word "The." The insertion point appears at the beginning of that paragraph—the paragraph you want to indent.

2 Click the **Increase Indent** button on the Formatting toolbar. Each time you click the Increase Indent button, Word indents text by 1/4 inch. As you see here, the paragraph is now indented. ■

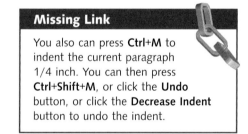

Missing Link

You also can press **Ctrl+M** to indent the current paragraph 1/4 inch. You can then press **Ctrl+Shift+M**, or click the **Undo** button, or click the **Decrease Indent** button to undo the indent.

Creating Bulleted and Numbered Lists

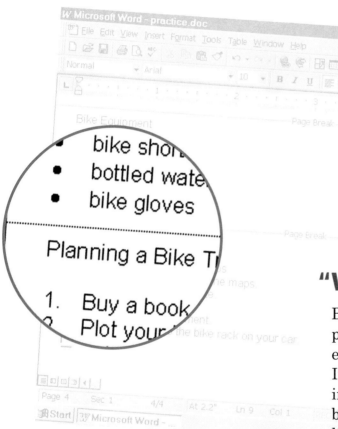

"Why would I do this?"

Bulleted and numbered lists help you present a series of ideas that help readers visually follow a document's path. If, for example, you type a list containing three items, you can have Word add bullets or numbers to the items in the list.

Bulleted lists are useful for presenting a series of parallel items that can be given in any order. Numbered lists are useful for presenting a set of items or steps that *must* be in a particular order.

1 Press **Ctrl+End** or scroll to the bottom of the document.

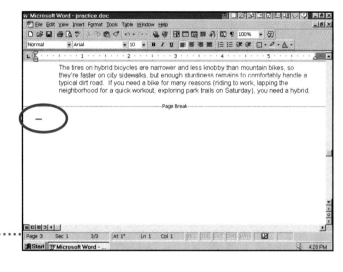

2 On page 3, type the text that appears in this figure. When you finish, your computer screen should match the one shown here.

3 When you have entered all of the information into your document, select the text to which you want to add bullets. For this example, select all of the lines of text except the first one.

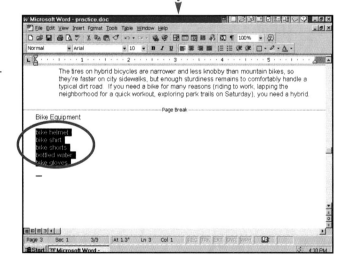

4 Click the **Bullets** button on the Formatting toolbar, and Word turns the selected lines of text into a bulleted list.

5 Click outside the selected text to deselect it. Now you can see the bulleted list better.

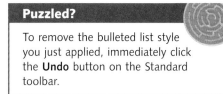

Puzzled?

To remove the bulleted list style you just applied, immediately click the **Undo** button on the Standard toolbar.

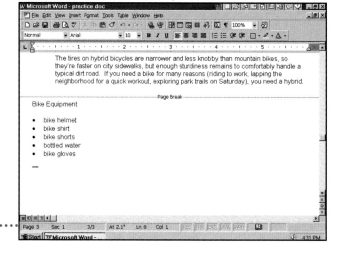

6 Press **Ctrl+End** or scroll to the bottom of the document. Then press **Ctrl+Enter** to insert a page break.

7 On page 4, type the text that appears in this figure. When you finish, your computer screen should match the one shown here.

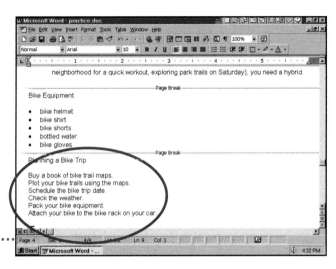

8 To create a numbered list, you must first select the text that you want to add numbers to. For this example, select all of the lines of text except the first one.

9 Click the **Numbering** button on the Formatting toolbar, and Word turns the selected text into a numbered list. Click outside the selected text to deselect it so you can see the numbered list better. ■

Puzzled?

To remove the numbered list style you just applied, immediately click the **Undo** button on the Standard toolbar.

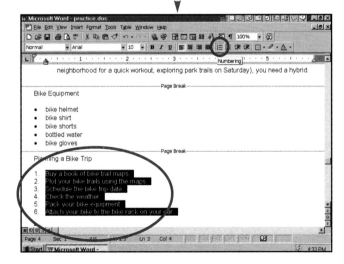

Setting Tabs and Margins

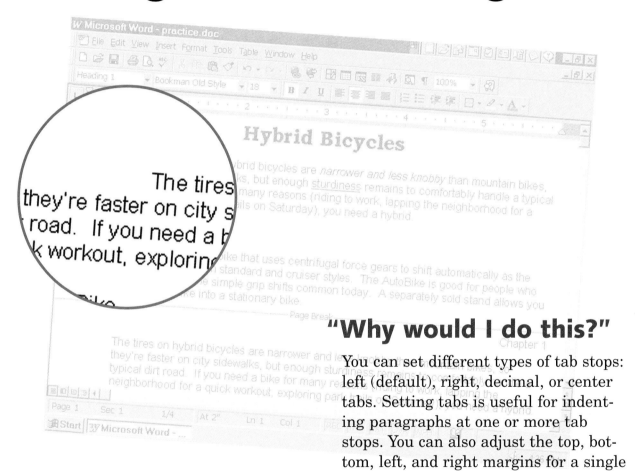

"Why would I do this?"

You can set different types of tab stops: left (default), right, decimal, or center tabs. Setting tabs is useful for indenting paragraphs at one or more tab stops. You can also adjust the top, bottom, left, and right margins for a single paragraph or a single page. For example, you might need to change the margins for two or three paragraphs that make up a long quotation, which needs to be set off from the rest of the text.

1 Place the insertion point at the beginning of the paragraph for which you want to set a tab. On page 1, click before the *T* in "The" at the beginning of the first paragraph.

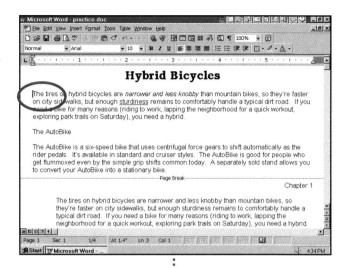

Missing Link

Word provides a default tab stop every 1/2 inch. Each time you press the Tab key on the keyboard, Word moves your text to the next 1/2-inch tab stop.

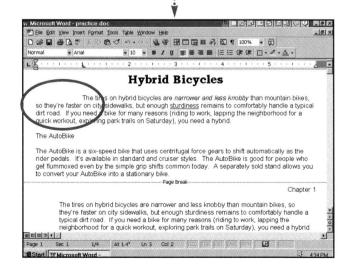

2 At the left end of the Ruler is the Tab Alignment button (with the letter L on it, which stands for Left tab). You want to set a left tab, so click below the number **1** on the Ruler to insert a tab marker (in this case, the letter L) under the number 1.

Missing Link

Click the **Tab Alignment** button to choose the type of tab stop you want: left (default), center, right, or decimal.

3 Press the **Tab** key to insert a tab and move the insertion point to the next tab stop. As you can see, the first sentence in the paragraph now starts one inch from the left margin.

Puzzled?

If you want to remove the tab stop, select the text for which you set the tab, point to the tab marker, and drag it off the Ruler. Then start over. Or, drag the tab marker to a new location on the Ruler.

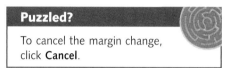

4 To change an existing tab stop, open the **File** menu and click **Page Setup**. You see the Page Setup dialog box. By default, the Margins tab is displayed. You see text boxes for each of the four margins—Top, Bottom, Left, and Right—and the Top entry is selected.

Puzzled?

To cancel the margin change, click **Cancel**.

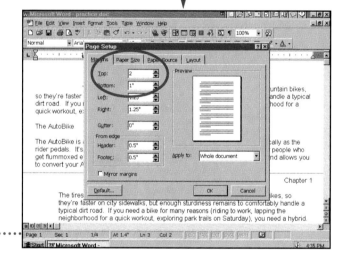

5 Type **2** in the **Top** text box and click **OK**. Word accepts the new margin setting and closes the dialog box.

6 Press **Ctrl+Home** to move the insertion point to the top of the document. The document now has a 2-inch top margin, as indicated in the status bar. ■

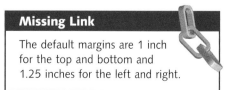

Missing Link

The default margins are 1 inch for the top and bottom and 1.25 inches for the left and right.

Numbering Pages and Creating Headers and Footers

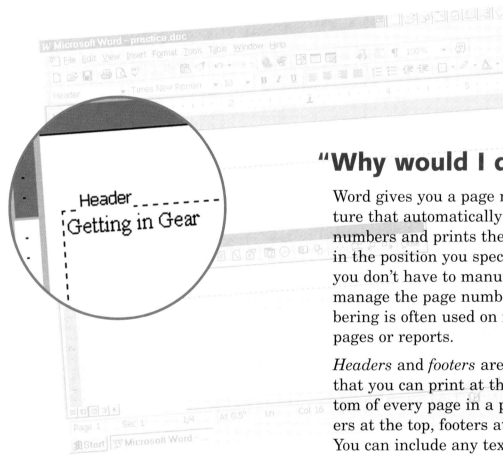

"Why would I do this?"

Word gives you a page numbering feature that automatically inserts page numbers and prints the page numbers in the position you specify. That way, you don't have to manually enter and manage the page numbers. Page numbering is often used on manuscript pages or reports.

Headers and *footers* are lines of text that you can print at the top and bottom of every page in a print job—headers at the top, footers at the bottom. You can include any text, page numbers, or the current date and time, and you can even format the information in a header and footer.

Task 28: Numbering Pages and Creating Headers and Footers

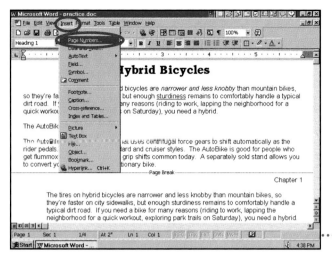

1 Open the **Insert** menu and click **Page Numbers**. Word opens the Page Numbers dialog box. The default page number position is Bottom of Page (Footer), and the default alignment is right.

2 Click the **Alignment** drop-down arrow, and Word displays a drop-down list of alignment choices. Choose **Center** to have Word center the page number on every page.

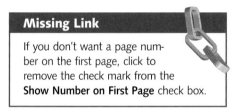

Missing Link

If you don't want a page number on the first page, click to remove the check mark from the **Show Number on First Page** check box.

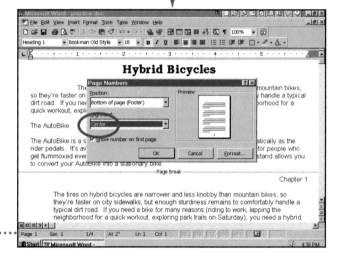

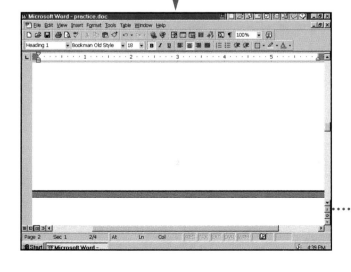

3 Click **OK**. Word creates a footer, adds the center-aligned page number to the footer, and switches to Page Layout view. Scroll to the bottom of page 2 to see the centered page number. (You can see the page number, header, and footer only when you're in Page Layout view or Print Preview, as explained in Part 5.)

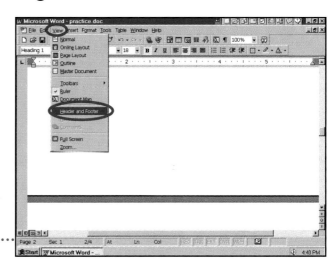

4 When you're in a view in which the header and footer are not displayed, you can view them by opening the **View** menu and clicking **Header and Footer**. Word displays the Header area and the Header and Footer toolbar.

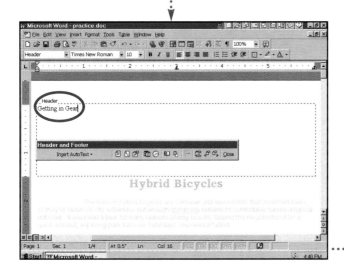

5 Type the text you want to print at the top of each page. For example, type **Getting in Gear** in the Header area. (If necessary, drag the Header and Footer toolbar by its title bar to a different area of the document so that you can see the Header area.)

6 Press **PgDn** or click the **Switch Between Header and Footer** button at the left end of the Header and Footer toolbar to move the insertion point to the Footer area.

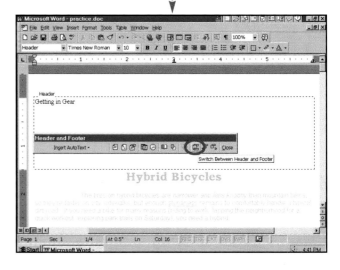

Task 28: Numbering Pages and Creating Headers and Footers

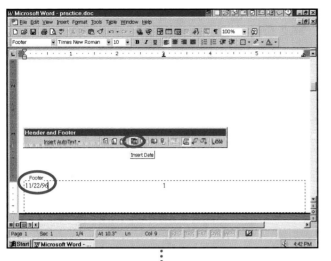

7 To include the date in the footer, click the **Insert Date** button on the Header and Footer toolbar. Word inserts the current date in the Footer area. That date will print at the bottom of each page.

Missing Link

Word provides several header and footer options for formatting the header or footer text. These options include bold, italic, underline, different fonts and font sizes, and text alignment.

8 Click the **Close Header and Footer** button on the Header and Footer toolbar to confirm the current header and footer and close the Footer window.

Puzzled?

If something unexpected prints at the top or bottom of your document, check the Header or Footer area. If you don't want a header or footer, select all the text in the Header or Footer area and press **Delete**.

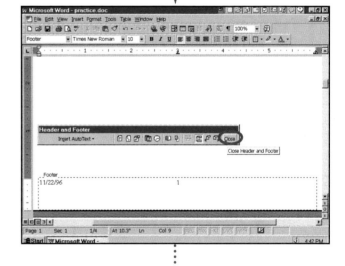

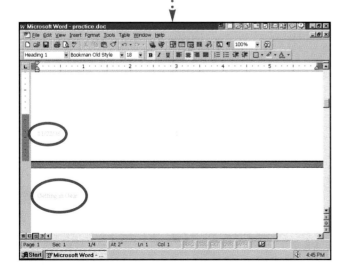

9 In Page Layout view, scroll to the bottom of page 1 so that you can see the footer on page 1 and the header at the top of page 2. ■

Inserting, Moving, and Resizing a Graphic

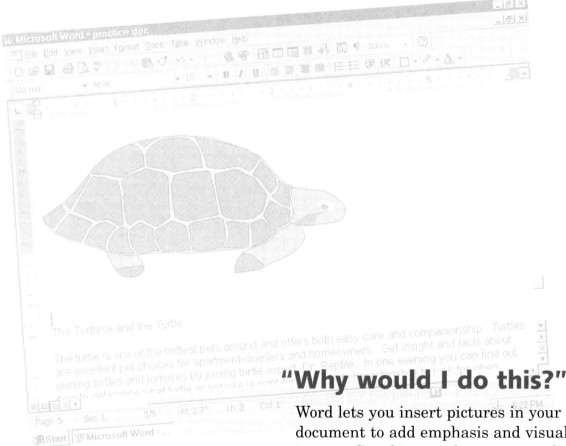

"Why would I do this?"

Word lets you insert pictures in your document to add emphasis and visual impact. Graphics can liven up any document. For example, if you were typing a newsletter article about tortoises and turtles, you could insert an animal graphic below the article.

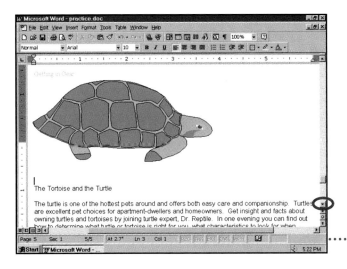

1 Press **Ctrl+End** or scroll to the bottom of the document. Then press **Ctrl+Enter** to insert a page break.

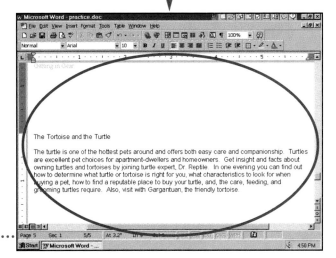

2 On page 5, type the text that appears in this figure. When you finish, your computer screen should match the one shown here.

3 Open the **Insert** menu, click **Picture**, and then click **Clip Art**. Word opens the Microsoft Clip Gallery dialog box.

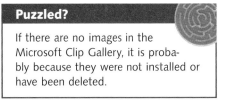

> **Puzzled?**
>
> If there are no images in the Microsoft Clip Gallery, it is probably because they were not installed or have been deleted.

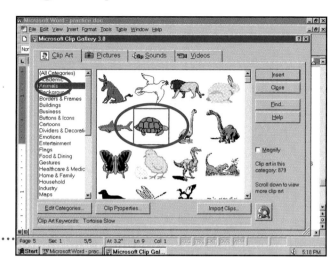

4 In the categories list (on the left), select the graphics category you want. For example, click **Animals**. Then click the green turtle picture located near the center of the dialog box.

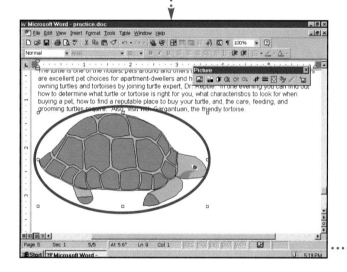

5 Click **Insert**, and Word places the graphic on-screen in the default position and size. You can change the picture's position and size.

6 The graphic is already selected so you can move it. Selection *handles* appear along the sides of the picture. Handles are the boxes at the corners and sides of the frame. Click and hold down the mouse button and drag the graphic above the heading. Release the mouse button.

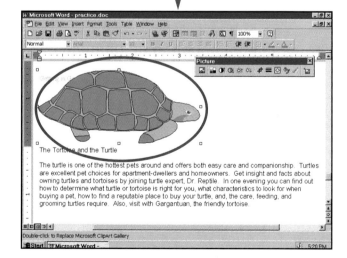

Puzzled?

To delete the graphic, click the graphic to select it and then press **Delete**.

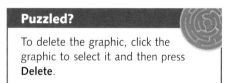

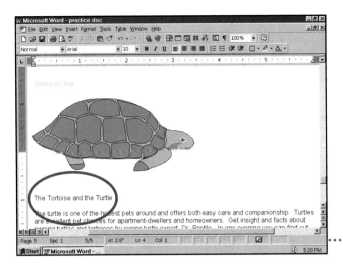

7 Click before the *T* in the word "The" in the heading and press **Enter** three times. This inserts space between the graphic and the heading.

8 Click the graphic to select it. To resize the graphic, move the mouse pointer to the top middle selection handle. When the mouse pointer changes to a double-headed arrow, drag the graphic down about 1/2 inch. This makes a graphic taller.

> **Puzzled?**
>
> Follow the same procedures to move the picture back to its original location or to change the picture back to its original size.

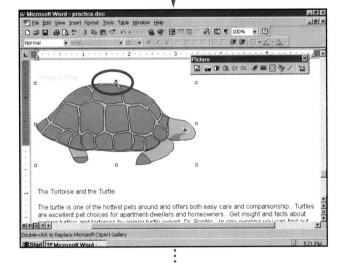

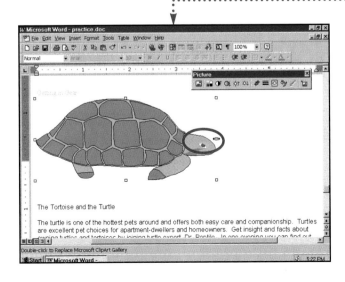

9 Move the mouse pointer to the right middle selection handle, and when the mouse pointer changes to a double-headed arrow, drag the graphic to the right about one inch. This makes the graphic wider. Click outside the graphic to deselect it. ■

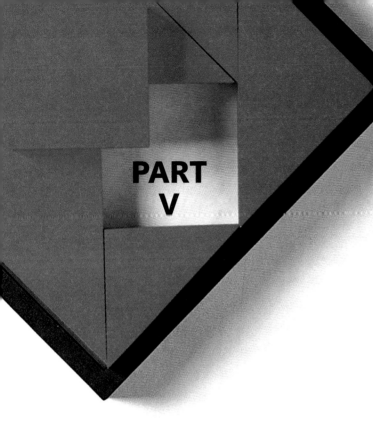

PART V

Viewing and Printing the Word Document

N THIS PART, YOU LEARN HOW TO CHANGE the view of your document, preview your document, and then print your document.

Word provides four views for your document: Normal, Outline, Page Layout, and Online Layout. Normal is the standard editing view you've been using. Outline view helps you create outlines. Page Layout view enables you to display multiple columns, headers and footers, and footnotes as they will be printed. Online Layout shows you how an Office document will look on the Internet as a Web page (large text that is wrapped more).

Word's Zoom feature works with any view. It lets you enlarge or reduce the view of a page on-screen. You can make text on the screen appear smaller or larger; it may show the whole page or a smaller section of it at higher magnification.

Print Preview is a view, but it's separate from the other views. With Word's Print Preview feature, you can review the appearance of the printed document before you produce the final output. (You can't edit in Print Preview.) The first page of the document appears in Print Preview as a reduced image in the Print Preview screen. You can use the Zoom feature to magnify the view.

In Word, you can print your documents using a basic printing procedure, or you can enhance the printout using several page setup options (as explained in Part IV). The Print dialog box lets you print some or all of the pages within a document, the current page, a range of pages, or selected text, and it gives you the option of printing multiple copies of the document.

The first time you use your printer with Word, it is a good idea to check the Setup options. Word can use the options and capabilities that are available with each printer. Often, you will need to provide more details about your printer so that Word knows its capabilities. If you want to specify details about your printer, choose the **File**, **Print** command and click the **Properties** button. Then you can confirm that you installed the right printer and connected it correctly, or you can switch to a different printer.

In this part, you learn how to print your document from the Print dialog box. But if you have already set up your print options and returned to the document, you can just click the **Print** button on the Standard toolbar to print your document.

This part introduces you to the basics of printing the document. With some experimentation and practice, you will be able to create some very interesting print results.

Zooming the Document

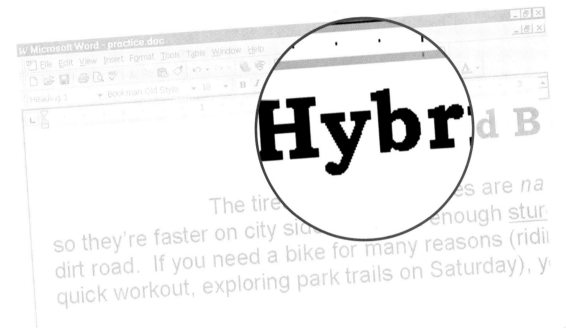

"Why would I do this?"

If you want to zoom in and get a closer look at text in your document, you select a higher percentage of magnification. For instance, if you work with small font sizes, you can inspect your text more closely without having to preview or print the document. On the other hand, if you want to zoom out so that more of the page—or even the whole page—shows on the screen at one glance, select a lower percentage of magnification.

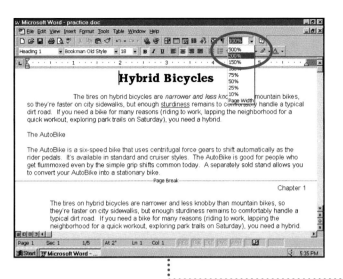

1 Press **Ctrl+Home** to go to the beginning of the document if necessary. Then click the **Zoom Control** drop-down arrow on the Standard toolbar and select **200%**. Word enlarges the document to a magnification of 200 percent.

Puzzled?

If you select the wrong magnification percentage, just switch to the percentage you want.

2 To see how a document looks when reduced to a size smaller than normal, click the **Zoom Control** drop-down arrow again. This time, select **50%**, and Word reduces the document to 50 percent its normal size.

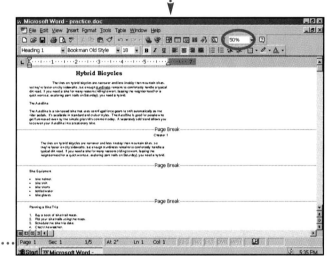

Puzzled?

If the percentage you want isn't listed, you can type it directly into the **Zoom Control** text box.

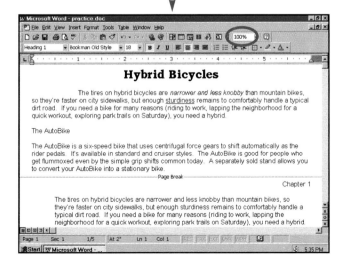

3 Click the **Zoom Control** drop-down arrow and click **100%** to restore the worksheet to 100 percent. ∎

Missing Link

To enlarge the document to completely fill the screen horizontally, select **Page Width** from the Zoom Control box.

Previewing the Document

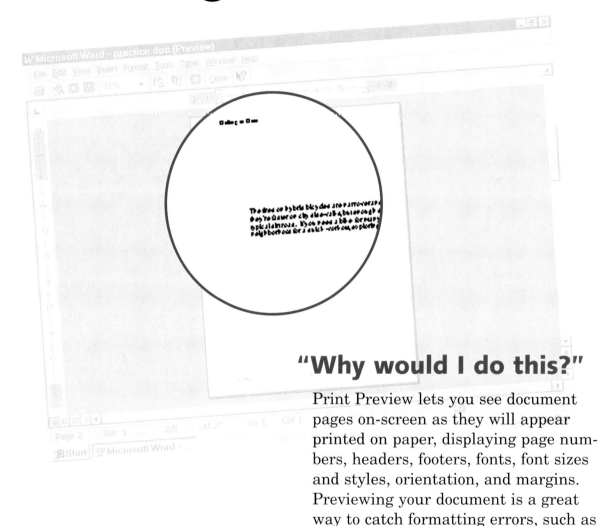

"Why would I do this?"

Print Preview lets you see document pages on-screen as they will appear printed on paper, displaying page numbers, headers, footers, fonts, font sizes and styles, orientation, and margins. Previewing your document is a great way to catch formatting errors, such as incorrect margins, overlapped text, and bold text that shouldn't be bold. You will save costly printer paper and time by previewing your document before you print.

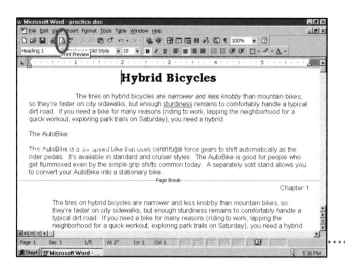

1 Click the **Print Preview** button on the Standard toolbar. This selects the Print Preview command.

2 You see a preview of how your document looks when printed. Click the **Next Page** button at the bottom of the vertical scroll bar to see the next page of your document.

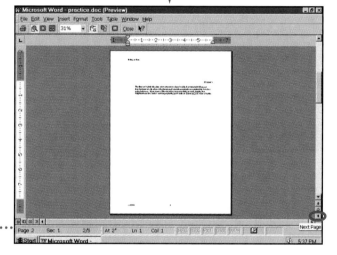

3 Move the mouse pointer around page 2. The mouse pointer (usually an arrow) changes to a magnifying glass with a plus sign (+). This mouse pointer lets you magnify any portion of the page.

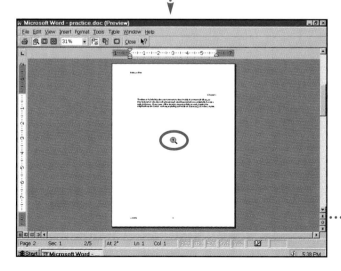

Missing Link

The Zoom Control box on the Print Preview toolbar lets you specify how large or small a document appears on the screen.

4 Click the header text at the top of the page. This zooms in on the top portion of your page and magnifies the text at 100 percent (as shown in the Zoom Control box). Notice that the mouse pointer becomes a magnifying glass with a minus sign (–). This mouse pointer lets you zoom out and shrink the text on the page.

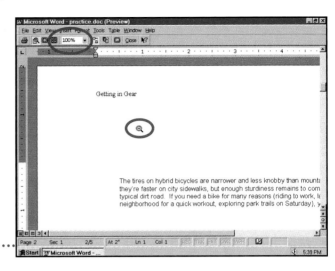

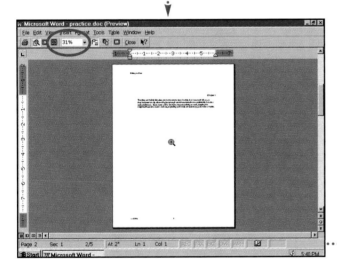

5 Click the text again, and the text returns to the normal 31 percent magnification.

6 To exit Print Preview, click the **Close Preview** button or press the **Esc** key. You're returned to your document. ■

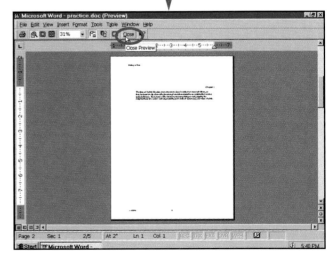

Printing the Document

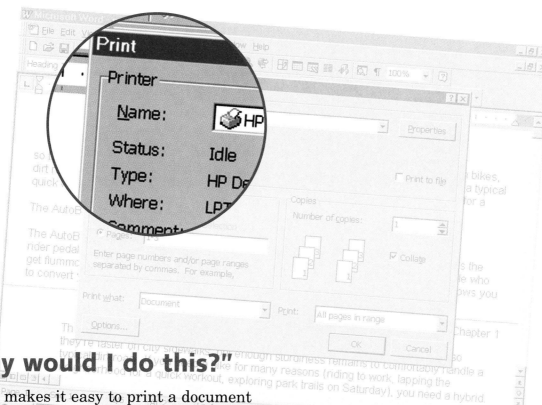

"Why would I do this?"

Word makes it easy to print a document and allows you to select the printer and font settings. You can print a single page, specific page ranges, specific separate pages, or selected text. You also can specify the number of copies, and you can collate the copies as you print. You might print a document that you need to give to others or that you need to file for reference.

Task 32: Printing the Document

1 Click the **Normal View** button at the left end of the horizontal scroll bar if you're not in Normal view. Then open the **File** menu and click **Print**, and Word opens the Print dialog box. This dialog box contains options with which you control your print jobs.

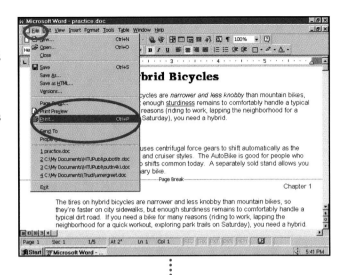

Missing Link

You can also press **Ctrl+P** to select the File Print command and open the Print dialog box.

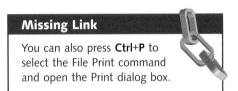

2 Choose any printing options you want. For example, select the **Pages** option and type **1–3** in the Pages text box. This tells Word to print pages 1 through 3.

Missing Link

To print disconnected pages, enter a comma between the page numbers and page ranges. For example, you could type 1,3,7,9–15,20.

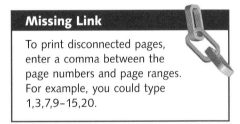

3 Click **OK** to start printing the document. ■

Missing Link

While the document is printing, Word displays a Printer icon at the right end of the Windows taskbar. Double-click the **Printer** icon to display the print queue dialog box. Then click the document name, open the **Document** menu, and click **Cancel Printing** to cancel the print job. Click the **Close** (X) button to close the dialog box.

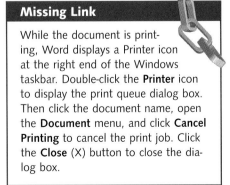

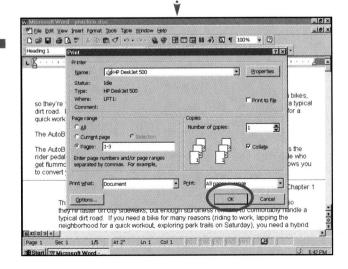

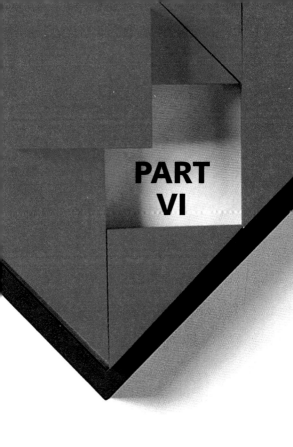

PART VI

Entering and Editing Data in Excel

WHEN YOU START THE PROGRAM, EXCEL DISPLAYS a blank *workbook*. The workbook is a file in which you store your data, similar to a three-ring binder. Within a workbook, you have *sheets*, such as *worksheets*, *chart sheets*, and *macro sheets*. A new workbook contains three sheets, named Sheet1 through Sheet3. You can have up to 255 sheets per workbook, depending on your computer's available memory. Multiple sheets help you organize, manage, and consolidate your data. For example, you might want to create a sales forecast for the first quarter of the year. Sheet1, Sheet2, and Sheet3 contain worksheet data for January, February, and March.

A worksheet is a grid of columns and rows. The intersection of any column and row is called a *cell*. Each cell in a worksheet has a unique cell reference. A cell reference is the designation formed by combining the row and column headings. For example, A8 is the reference of the cell at the intersection of column A and row 8. A worksheet contains 256 columns identified by the letters A through Z and then AA through IV. A worksheet contains 65,536 rows identified by the numbers 1 through 65536. The total number of cells on a worksheet is 16,777,216.

The *cell pointer* is a cross-shaped pointer that appears over cells in the worksheet. You use the cell pointer to select any cell in the worksheet. The selected cell is called the *active cell*. You have at least one cell selected at all times.

A *range* is a specified group of cells. A range can be a single cell, a column, a row, or any combination of cells, columns, and rows. *Range coordinates* identify a range. The first element in the range coordinates is the reference of the uppermost left cell in the range; the second element is the reference of the lowermost right cell. A colon (:) separates these two elements. The range A1:C3, for example, includes the cells A1, A2, A3, B1, B2, B3, C1, C2, and C3.

The worksheet is much larger than one screen can display. To place data in the many cells that make up the worksheet, you must be able to move to the desired locations. There are many ways to move around the worksheet (see the following table). When you move the cell pointer to a cell, that cell becomes the active cell. The active cell has a dark border around it.

To Move	Press
Right one cell or left one cell	→ or ←
Up one cell or down one cell	↑ or ↓
To the beginning of a row or the end of a row	Home or End+→
To the first (upper-left) cell (A1)	Ctrl+Home
To the last (bottom right) cell (containing data)	Ctrl+End

You can enter four types of data into an Excel worksheet: text, numbers, calculations, and dates. Text entries can contain letters, symbols, numbers, or any combination of these characters. Numeric entries contain numbers, dates, times, currency, percentages, text, and other symbols. Numeric entries must begin with a numeral or one of the following symbols: +, −, (, ., or $. If you want to left-align a text entry, a number, or an entry that begins with a number followed by text, type an apostrophe (') at the beginning of the entry.

Excel deals with dates as values. The following table shows the Excel formats you can use when entering a date in a cell, along with a sample of the result Excel will display:

Format	Example
MM/DD/YY	9/12/97
DD-MMM-YY	12-Sep-97
DD-MMM	12-Sep (assumes the current year)
MMM-YY	Sep-97 (assumes the first day of the month)

In this part, you also learn how to create and print a column chart.

TASK

33

Moving Around the Worksheet

"Why would I do this?"

Because you typically use many cells in a worksheet, you need shortcuts for moving around the worksheet. Using a mouse is often the easiest way to move around the worksheet; you use the vertical or horizontal scroll bar to see other portions of the worksheet. However, you can also use the keyboard to move around. And with Excel's Go To command, you can quickly jump to cells that are out of view.

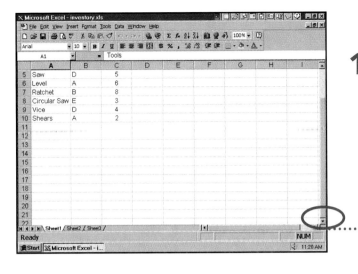

1 Start Excel (see Task 1: "Starting and Exiting Microsoft Office 97 Programs"). In the worksheet, click four times on the down scroll arrow at the bottom of the vertical scroll bar. Excel moves the worksheet down one row at a time, so after the fourth click, row 5 appears at the top of the worksheet.

2 Click three times on the up scroll arrow at the top of the vertical scroll bar, and Excel scrolls the worksheet up one row at a time. Therefore, after you click three times, row 2 appears at the top of the worksheet.

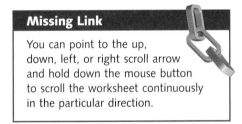

Missing Link

You can point to the up, down, left, or right scroll arrow and hold down the mouse button to scroll the worksheet continuously in the particular direction.

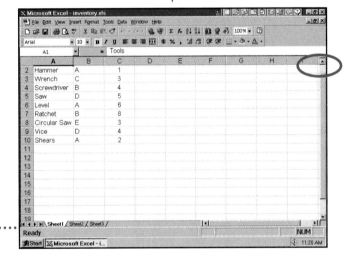

3 Drag the scroll box up to the top of the vertical scroll bar. This moves the worksheet quickly to a new location in the direction you drag the scroll box.

Missing Link

When you drag a scroll box, a ScreenTip indicates the current location of the scroll box with the row number or column letter.

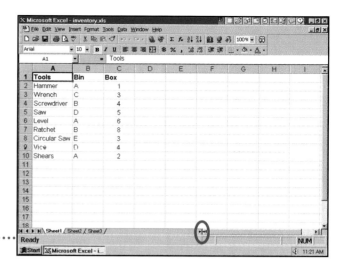

4 Point to the tab split box (the vertical bar located to the left of the left horizontal scroll arrow). The mouse pointer changes to a vertical bar with a left and a right arrow.

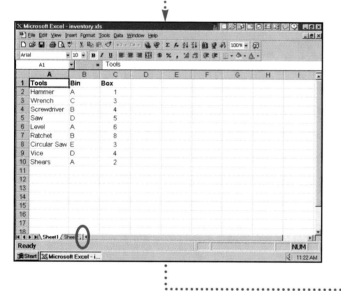

5 Drag the tab split box to the left until the box is aligned with the right edge of the Sheet2 tab. In this case, you see the Sheet1 and Sheet2 tabs and more of the horizontal scroll bar.

> **Puzzled?**
>
> If you run out of room to move the mouse on your desktop or mouse pad, just lift the mouse and then put it down.

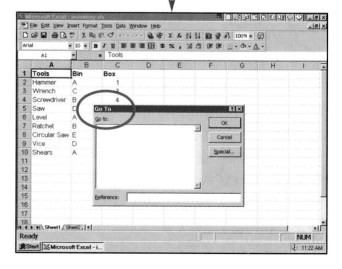

6 Press **F5**, the Go To key, to select the Go To command. Excel displays the Go To dialog box, with the insertion point is in the Reference text box.

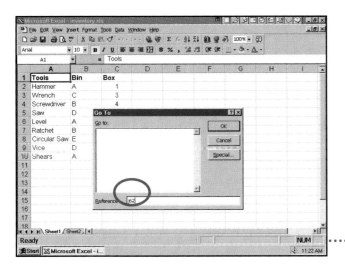

7 Enter the cell to which you want to go. For this example, type **j62**. (Remember that a cell is referenced by its column letter and row number.)

8 Press **Enter**, and Excel moves the cell pointer to cell J62, making it the active cell. The cell reference appears in the Name text box below the Font box on the Formatting toolbar. ▪

Puzzled?

If you mistakenly move to the wrong cell, repeat the Go To command to move to the correct cell.

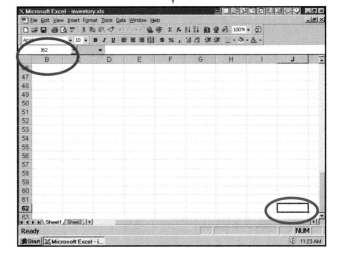

TASK 34

Moving Between Worksheets

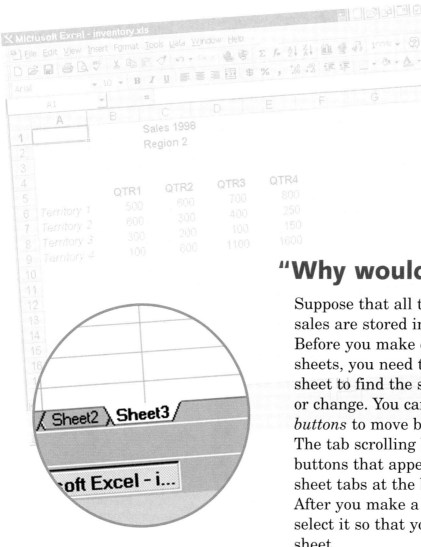

"Why would I do this?"

Suppose that all the sheets relating to sales are stored in one workbook. Before you make changes to these sheets, you need to move from sheet to sheet to find the sheet you want to view or change. You can use the *tab scrolling buttons* to move between worksheets. The tab scrolling buttons are the four buttons that appear to the left of the sheet tabs at the bottom of the screen. After you make a sheet visible, you can select it so that you can work on the sheet.

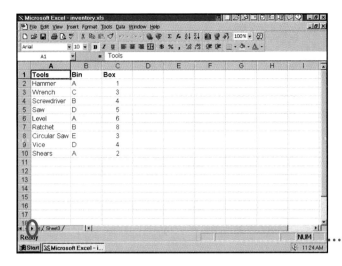

1 To the left of the sheet tabs, click the **Next Tab** scrolling button (the third button from the left) twice. Each time you click, Excel scrolls the sheets to display one more sheet tab to the right. In this case, clicking the button twice hides the Sheet1 and Sheet2 tabs and displays the Sheet3 tab.

2 Double-click the **Previous Tab** scrolling button (the second button from the left). Each time you click the Previous Tab scrolling button, Excel scrolls the sheets to display one more sheet tab to the left. In this case, clicking twice redisplays the Sheet1 and Sheet2 tabs.

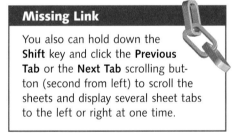

Missing Link

You also can hold down the **Shift** key and click the **Previous Tab** or the **Next Tab** scrolling button (second from left) to scroll the sheets and display several sheet tabs to the left or right at one time.

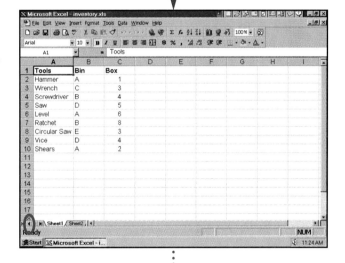

3 Click the **Last Tab** scrolling button (the rightmost button), and Excel displays the last sheet tab in the workbook. Notice that, in this case, the last sheet tab is Sheet3.

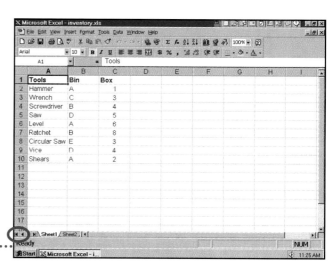

4 Click the **First Tab** scrolling button (the leftmost button), and Excel displays the first sheet tab in the workbook. In this case, Excel redisplays the Sheet1 and Sheet2 tabs.

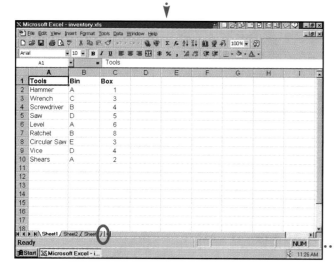

5 To make room for more sheet tabs to appear, drag the tab split box to the right until the box is aligned with the right edge of the Sheet3 tab. This enables you to see more sheet tabs (the Sheet1, Sheet2, and Sheet3 tabs are now visible) and less of the horizontal scroll bar.

6 You can click any of the tabs to make a sheet active. For example, click the **Sheet3** tab, and Excel moves that sheet to the top and makes it the active sheet.

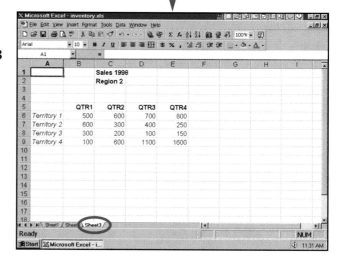

Puzzled?

If you accidentally move to the wrong sheet, click the appropriate tab scrolling button to move to the sheet you want to view in the workbook. If you selected the wrong sheet, just click the correct sheet tab.

Selecting Cells

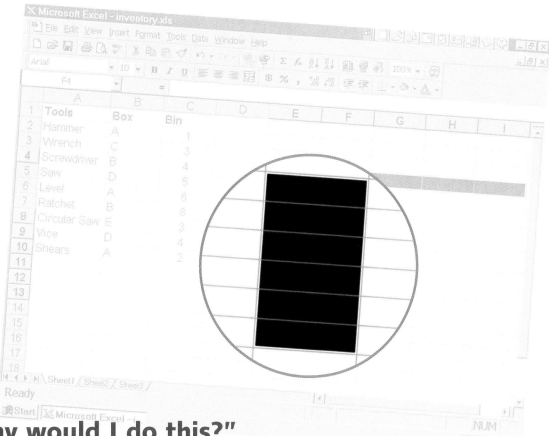

"Why would I do this?"

Knowing how to select a cell is essential because most of the commands and options you choose in Excel affect the selected cell. You also can select a *range*—a group of adjacent cells on which to perform some action. You can even select several ranges at one time with the mouse.

For example, you may want to perform a command on a group of cells that are not adjacent. Maybe you want to change the alignment of text in the top row of the worksheet and a column along the side. To make the change to both ranges, you need to select both ranges at the same time.

Task 35: Selecting Cells

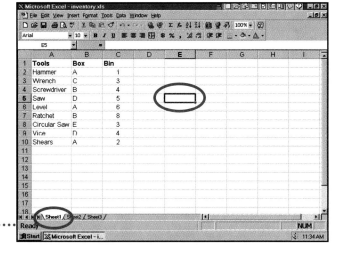

1 Click the **Sheet1** tab to select Sheet1. Then click cell **E5**, and it becomes the active cell.

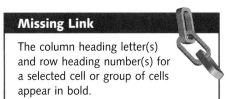

Missing Link

The column heading letter(s) and row heading number(s) for a selected cell or group of cells appear in bold.

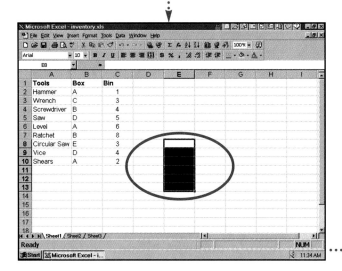

2 Hold down the mouse button and drag across cells **E8**, **E9**, **E10**, **E11**, **E12**, and **E13** to select them. This deselects cell E5 and selects the range E8:E13.

Puzzled?

If you select the wrong cell, simply click the correct cell. If you select the wrong range, click any cell to deselect the range.

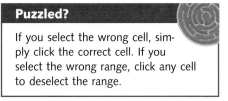

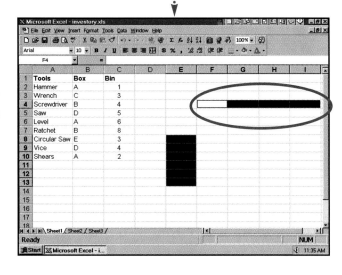

3 To select another range of cells, hold down the **Ctrl** key and drag across cells **G4**, **H4**, and **I4**. Release the mouse button and then the **Ctrl** key. Notice that the first range (E8:E13) remains selected, and the second range G4:I4 also is selected.

Entering Text and Numbers

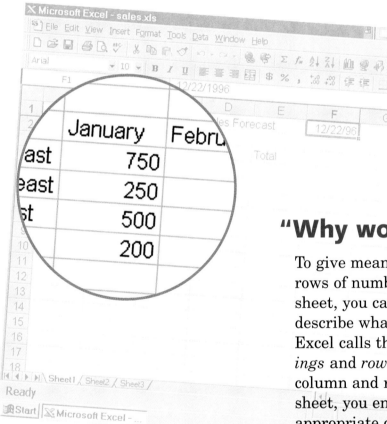

"Why would I do this?"

To give meaning to the columns and rows of numbers that make up a worksheet, you can give them names to describe what the numbers represent. Excel calls these names *column headings* and *row headings*. After you add column and row headings to the worksheet, you enter numbers into the appropriate cells. Excel also lets you enter dates and times in a worksheet.

In this task, create a sales forecast worksheet for the first three months of the year. Enter headings that describe the worksheet, specify time periods, and identify several sales territories. Then enter the sales data.

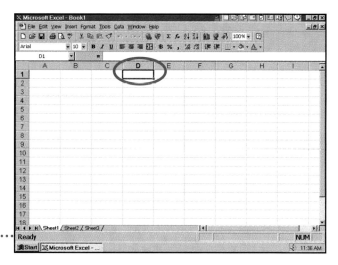

1 Press **Ctrl+Home** to move to the top of the worksheet. Then click cell **D1** to make it the active cell. (The active cell on a worksheet has a bold border.) When the mouse pointer is within the worksheet, the pointer appears as a cross.

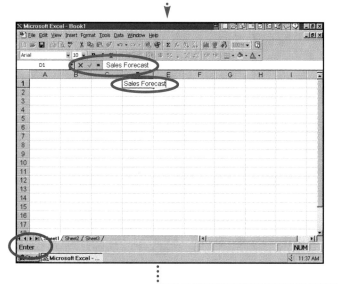

2 Type **Sales Forecast** as the title of your worksheet. As you type, the entry appears in the Formula bar and in the active cell. The mode indicator in the lower-left corner of the screen displays Enter.

> **Missing Link**
>
> An X button and a check mark button appear to the left of the entry in the Formula bar. You can click the X to cancel your change, or click the check mark to confirm the new entry.

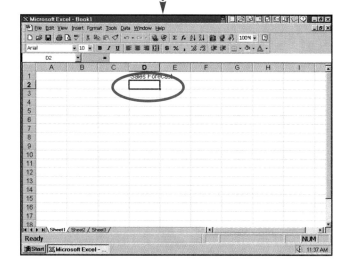

3 Press **Enter**. Excel accepts the entry in the Formula bar, enters it into the cell, and makes the next cell down (cell D2) the active cell. Notice that "Sales Forecast" is left-aligned.

> **Missing Link**
>
> Excel always moves down one cell when you type data and press Enter.

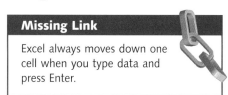

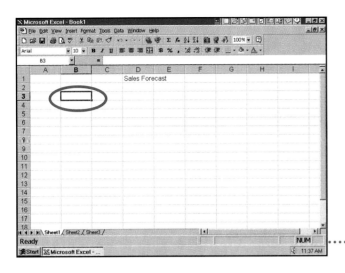

4 Next, select cell **B3**, the cell in which you want to enter a title that will be the first column heading.

5 Type **January** and press the right arrow key (→). Excel accepts the entry, enters the title into the cell, and makes the cell to the right (cell C3) the active cell.

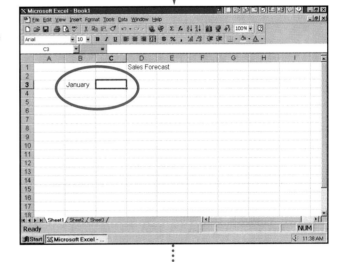

Puzzled?

If you make a mistake when typing an entry, use the **Backspace** key to correct the entry. Excel does not place the entry in the cell until you press Enter, press an arrow key, or click the check mark in the Formula bar.

6 Type **February** and press the right arrow key (→), and then type **March** and press the right arrow key (→). When you finish, cell E3 is the active cell.

7 Type **Total** and press **Enter**. Then click cell **A4** and start typing the remaining data shown in this figure. When you finish, your computer screen should match the one shown here.

> **Puzzled?**
>
> To delete the most recent entry, select the **Edit**, **Undo Entry** command or click the **Undo** button on the Standard toolbar.

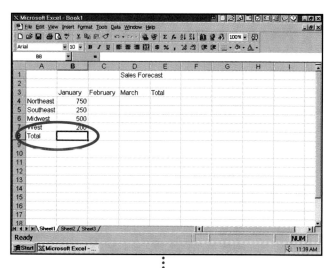

8 Click cell **F1** and type **12/22/96**. Then click the check mark button in the Formula bar. Excel accepts the entry and enters the date in the cell (right-aligned). Note that when you use the check mark button in the Formula bar, Excel does not move the cell pointer to another cell. Therefore, in this figure, cell F1 remains the active cell.

9 Click the **Save** button on the Standard toolbar to save this spreadsheet. In the **Name** text box, enter the name **SALES**. (Excel automatically adds the .XLS extension.) The file name SALES.XLS appears in the title bar. ■

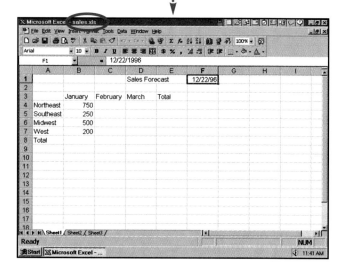

Overwriting a Cell and Erasing a Cell

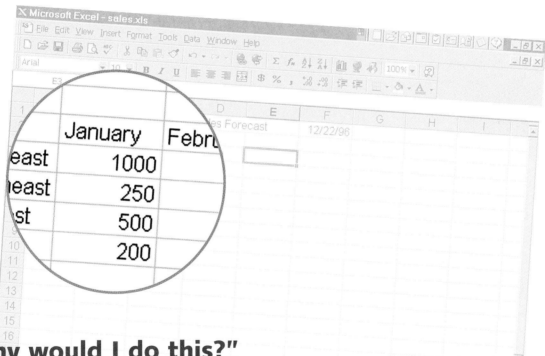

"Why would I do this?"

Overwriting a cell means to replace the existing contents of a cell with new data. Overwriting a cell is handy when you want to correct typing errors or when a cell contains wrong data. When you overwrite, all data in the cell is deleted as soon as you begin entering new data.

You can easily erase the contents of a cell by using the Delete key. Erasing a

cell is useful when you change your mind about the contents after you press Enter and Excel enters the data in the cell. Sometimes you may find that a piece of data you've already typed in a cell is incorrect and needs to be changed. Instead of editing the cell to remove the entry, you can erase the cell's contents with the Delete key and then start over.

1 Click cell **B4** to make it the active cell. The Formula bar displays the current entry—the entry you want to overwrite. The mode indicator (at the left end of the status bar) displays Ready.

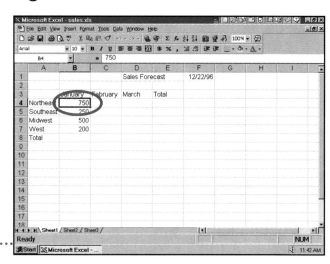

2 Type **1000**. The number 1000 becomes the new entry in the cell and appears in the Formula bar.

Missing Link

Be careful not to accidentally overwrite formulas. If you overwrite a formula with a constant value, Excel will no longer update the formula. (If you do accidentally overwrite a formula but you've saved your spreadsheet recently, you can reopen the spreadsheet and try again.)

3 Press **Enter**. Excel replaces the previous entry with the new entry, and then moves down to cell B5, making it the active cell. (Until you press Enter, you can press the Esc key at any time to cancel the changes.)

Puzzled?

If you make a mistake when typing the entry, use the Backspace key to correct it. Excel does not place the entry in the cell until you press Enter or an arrow key.

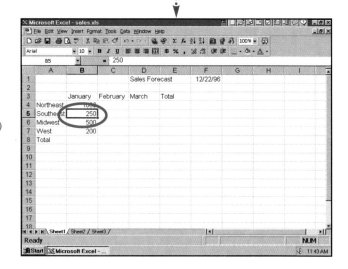

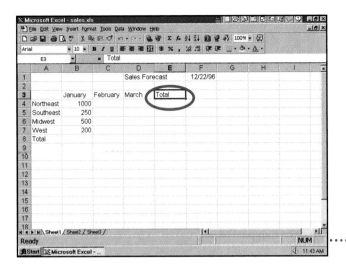

4 To erase a cell entry, select the cell whose contents you want to erase. For example, click cell **E3** to make it the active cell. The Formula bar displays the current entry—the entry you want to erase.

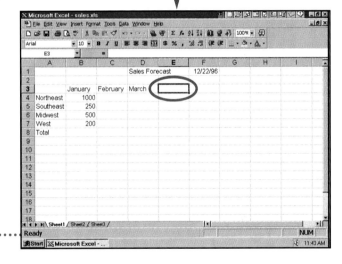

5 Press **Delete**. When you press the Delete key, Excel deletes the entry from the cell but leaves the formatting.

6 To restore a cell's contents that you just deleted, click the **Undo** button on the Standard toolbar. Excel restores the entry. ■

Missing Link

You also can use the Delete key to delete data in a range of cells.

Editing a Cell

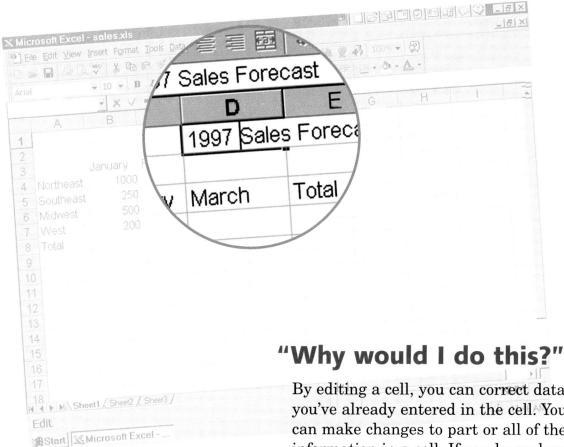

"Why would I do this?"

By editing a cell, you can correct data you've already entered in the cell. You can make changes to part or all of the information in a cell. If you know how to edit your data, you won't have to type an entire entry over again if it changes or you realize you've made a mistake. You can just make a few quick changes to correct the cell's contents. (However, if the new entry is entirely different, you would probably be better off to overwrite the entry instead as described in the previous task.)

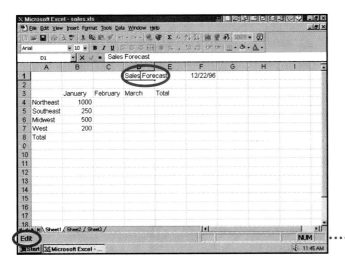

1 Place the insertion point in the cell whose entry you want to change. For example, double-click cell **D1**. The X button and the check mark button appear in the Formula bar, and the mode indicator at the left end of the status bar displays Edit.

2 Press **Home** to move the insertion point to the beginning of the entry.

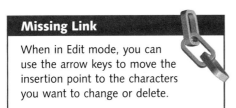

Missing Link

When in Edit mode, you can use the arrow keys to move the insertion point to the characters you want to change or delete.

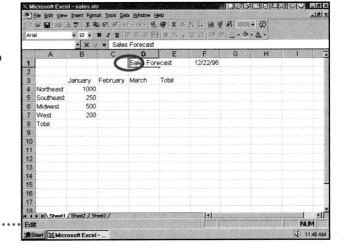

3 Type **1997** and press the **Spacebar**. As you type in Edit mode, Excel inserts the new characters at the location of the insertion point and moves existing characters to the right. This entry changes the title.

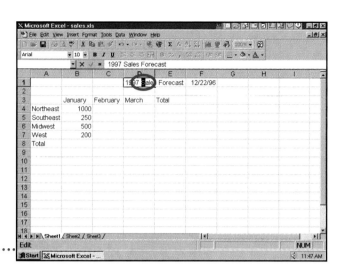

4 Press **Ins**. When you're in Edit mode and you press the Ins key, Excel switches gears, allowing you to overwrite existing characters. This step highlights the letter **S** (the character that the insertion point is on).

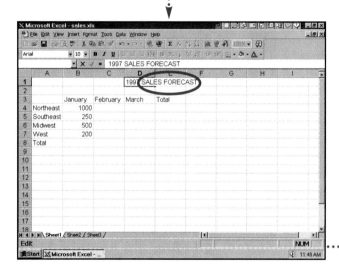

5 Type **SALES FORECAST**—using all capital letters—over the existing title. As you can see, this changes the lowercase letters in the title to uppercase letters.

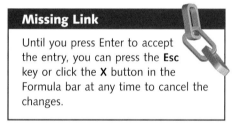

Missing Link

Until you press Enter to accept the entry, you can press the **Esc** key or click the **X** button in the Formula bar at any time to cancel the changes.

6 Press **Enter**. Excel accepts the new entry and moves down to make cell D2 the active cell. (Because the entry is too long to display in the column, Excel hides a portion of the title. In Task 40, you learn how to move the title to make it visible.) ▪

Puzzled?

Excel does not place the entry in the cell until you press Enter, press an arrow key, or click the check mark button in the Formula bar.

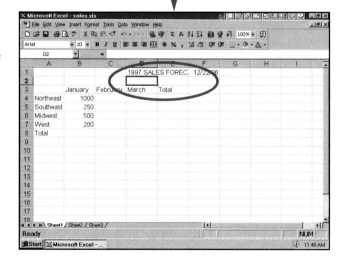

Copying a Cell

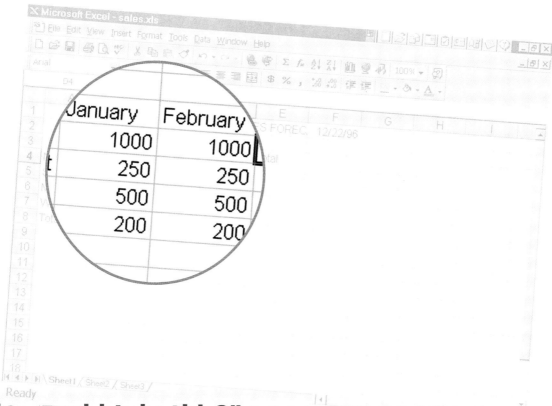

"Why would I do this?"

You can save the time of retyping information you need to repeat on a worksheet by copying a cell over and over again. You might, for example, want to copy a title or a value from one cell to another cell. That way you wouldn't have to type the title or value over again, which would save you time and keystrokes and decrease the risk that you might introduce errors.

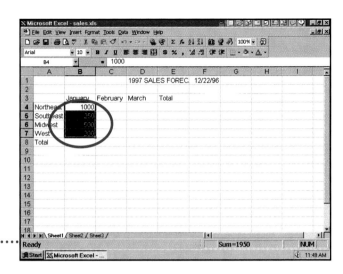

1 Select the entry you want to copy. For this example, click cell **B4** and drag downward to cell **B7**. This selects the range B4:B7; it appears highlighted.

2 Click the **Copy** button on the Standard toolbar, and a dashed *marquee* surrounds the cell or cells you are copying. The status bar briefly displays the message Copies selection onto Clipboard when you click on the Copy button.

3 Select the cell to which you want to copy the data. For example, select cell **C4** to make it the active cell. The status bar reminds you how to complete the task: Select destination and press ENTER or choose Paste.

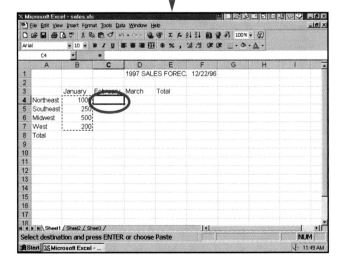

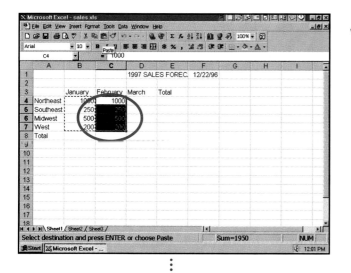

4 Click the **Paste** button on the Standard toolbar, and Excel pastes a copy of the data into the active cell. As you can see, the entry appears in cells C4 through C7. Note that Excel copies the entry *and* the format (alignment, protection settings, and so on).

Missing Link

You also can use the **Ctrl+C** and **Ctrl+V** key combinations to select the Copy and Paste commands, respectively.

5 The marquee remains around the range B4:B7 to tell you that if you choose to paste again, Excel will still use this selection. Press **Esc** to remove the copy marquee from the range B4:B7. ▪

Puzzled?

If you copy the wrong data or copy the data to the wrong location, click the **Undo** button on the Standard toolbar to undo the most recent copy.

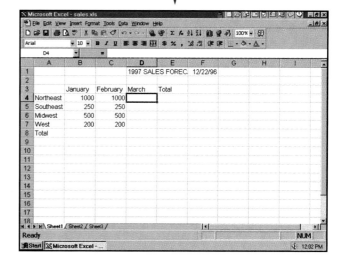

Moving a Cell

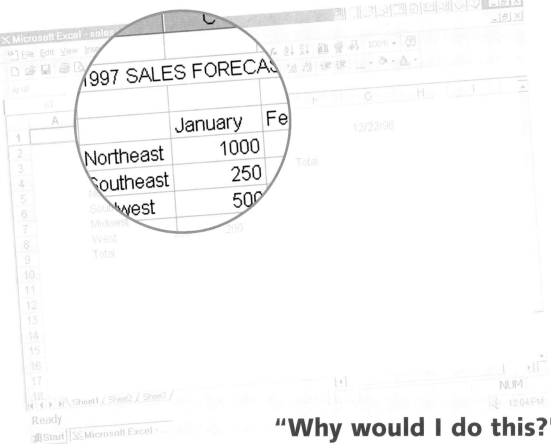

"Why would I do this?"

Excel's Move command lets you remove information from one cell and place it into another cell. This means you do not have to go to the new cell and enter the same data and then erase the data from the old location. For example, you might want to move data in a worksheet if the layout of the worksheet has changed.

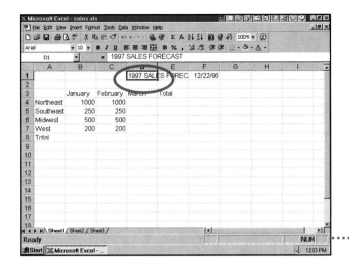

1 Select cell **D1** to make it the active cell. The Formula bar displays the current entry—the entry you want to move.

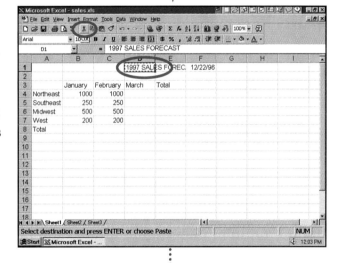

2 Click the **Cut** button on the Standard toolbar. Excel cuts the entry from its original location and places it in a temporary storage location called the Clipboard. A dashed marquee surrounds the cell whose contents you are cutting. The status bar briefly displays the message Cuts selection and places it onto Clipboard when you click on the Cut button.

3 Select the cell in which you want to place the entry. For this example, select cell **A1** to make it the active cell. The status bar reminds you how to complete the task: Select destination and press ENTER or choose Paste.

4 Click the **Paste** button on the Standard toolbar to paste the data into the cell. The entry appears in cell A1. Note that Excel moves the entry *and* the formatting (alignment, protection settings, and so on).

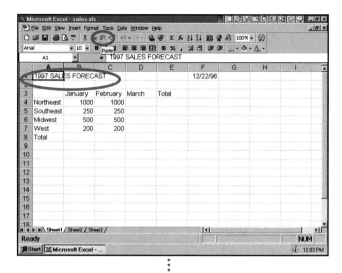

> ### Missing Link
>
> You also can use the **Ctrl+X** and **Ctrl+V** key combinations to select the Cut and Paste commands, respectively.

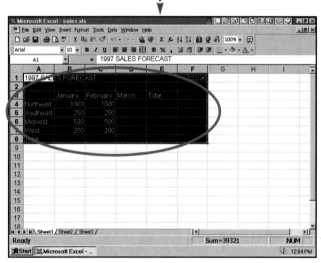

5 You can quickly move data in a range by dragging it. To do so, select the range whose data you want to move: **A1:F8**.

> ### Puzzled?
>
> If you move the wrong data or move the data to the wrong location, click the **Undo** button on the Standard toolbar to undo the most recent move. Then start over.

6 Position the mouse pointer over the selected range's bottom border. When the pointer changes to an arrow, drag down to row 9 and to the right into column G. When you release the mouse button, Excel moves the entire range to the new location. Click any cell to deselect the range. ■

> ### Puzzled?
>
> You can also position the mouse pointer in the upper-left corner of the destination area and click the **Paste** button. If the area already contains data, Excel asks if you want to replace its contents.

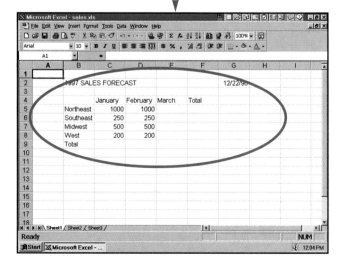

Filling a Range

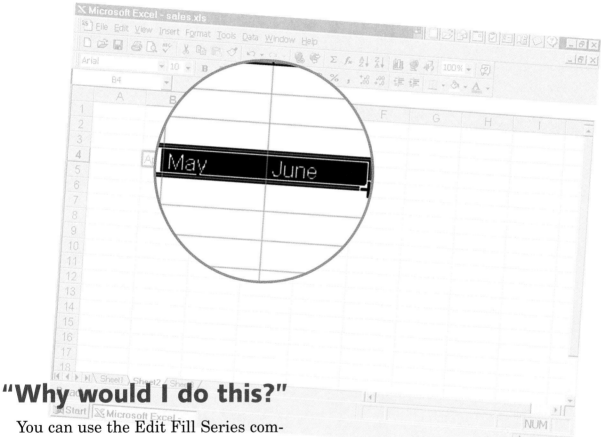

"Why would I do this?"

You can use the Edit Fill Series command to enter a series of numbers or dates. For example, you can type 100 in the first cell in a range and then fill in the rest of the range. Or you can drag to increment the number by 1, in which case Excel fills in the numbers 101, 102, 103, and so on. This command is useful for entering invoice numbers and ratings and to fill a range with the same text, numbers, and formulas.

Task 41: Filling a Range

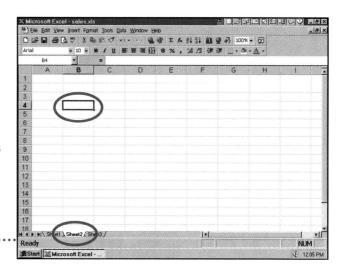

1 Click the **Sheet2** tab and then click cell **B4**. This selects Sheet2 and moves it to the top, making it the active sheet. B4 becomes the active cell, in which you will enter the first column title.

2 Type **April** and click the check mark button in the Formula bar. This enters the *start value* for the fill and indicates to Excel the type of series you want to use—in this case, months.

Missing Link

Excel automatically fills the range based on the data you enter in the first cell of the range.

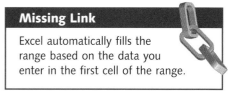

3 Move the mouse pointer to the fill handle at the lower-right corner of the current cell's border. When the mouse pointer changes to a black cross, drag the fill handle across cells **C4** and **D4**. When you release the mouse button, Excel fills the range with the next months in the series. ■

Puzzled?

To undo the fill series, click the **Undo** button on the Standard toolbar immediately after filling the range.

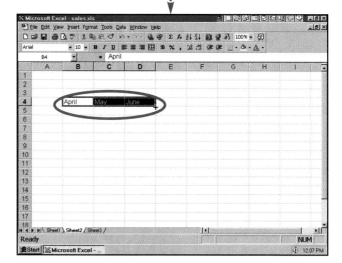

Inserting and Deleting Rows and Columns

"Why would I do this?"

You can insert extra rows and columns to make more room for additional data or formulas. Adding more space between rows and columns makes the worksheet easier to read. On the other hand, you might want to delete rows or columns from a worksheet to close up some empty space. In this task, you'll add a row to a worksheet and then delete a column.

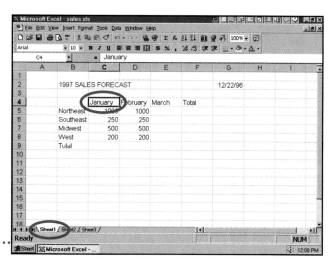

1 Click the **Sheet1** tab and click cell **C4**. Excel moves Sheet1 to the top and selects cell C4. You can select any cell in a row to tell Excel where you want to insert a new row. Excel will insert the new row above the row you select (row 4).

2 Open the **Insert** menu and click **Rows** to insert a new row above row 4. Excel automatically moves the other rows down to make room for the new one.

3 To select the column you want to delete, click the column heading at the top of column C. Be sure to click the column letter, not a cell in the column. This selects the entire column.

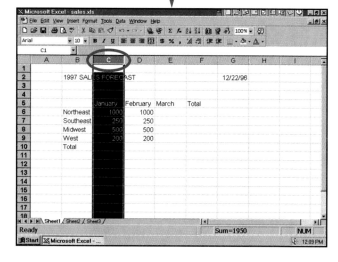

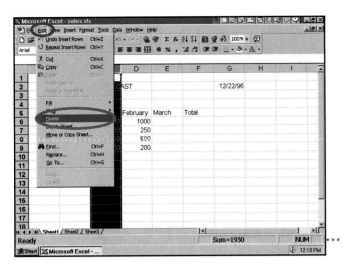

4 Open the **Edit** menu and click **Delete**.

Missing Link

If you see the Delete dialog box, you did not select the entire column. Click the **Entire Column** button and click **OK**.

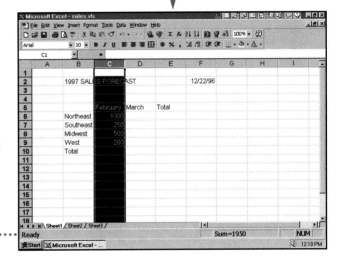

5 Excel immediately deletes the column and shifts all remaining columns that were to the right of column C left one column to fill the empty space.

6 Click the **Undo** button on the Standard toolbar. Excel restores the deleted column to its original location. Click any cell to deselect the range. ▨

Puzzled?

To undo a row or column insertion/deletion you've just made, click the **Undo** button on the Standard toolbar immediately.

Changing the View

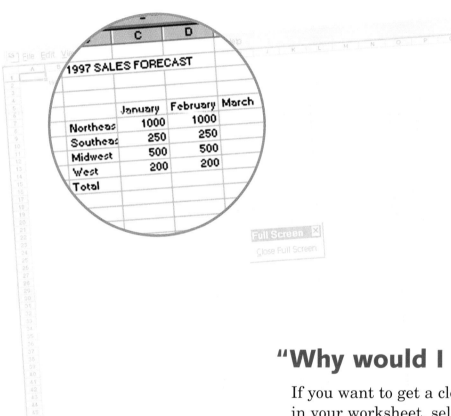

"Why would I do this?"

If you want to get a closer look at data in your worksheet, select a higher percentage of magnification. For instance, if you enter a title or value that appears to overlap the adjacent title or value, you can inspect this closely without having to preview or print the worksheet.

On the other hand, if you want to zoom out so that the whole worksheet shows on the screen at one glance, select a lower percentage of magnification. You can also save a spreadsheet view.

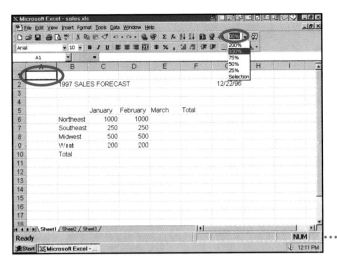

1 Click cell **A1** to move to the beginning of the worksheet. Then click the **Zoom Control** drop-down arrow on the Standard toolbar.

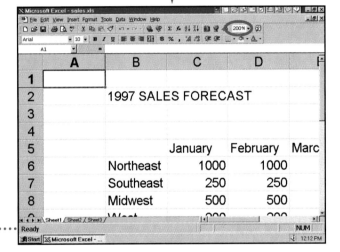

2 Click **200%** to enlarge the worksheet to a magnification of 200%. At this level, you can check the minute details of your worksheet.

3 To reduce the magnification so you can see most of the worksheet, click the **Zoom Control** drop-down arrow again and click **50%**. Excel reduces the worksheet to 50% of its normal size.

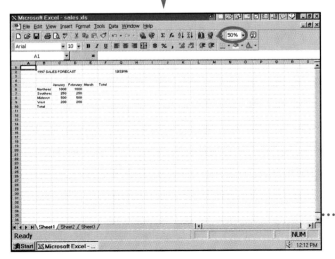

Puzzled?

If you select the wrong magnification percentage, just select a different percentage to switch to it. You can also select **Fit Selection** to have Excel reduce or enlarge a selection just enough to fit the current window.

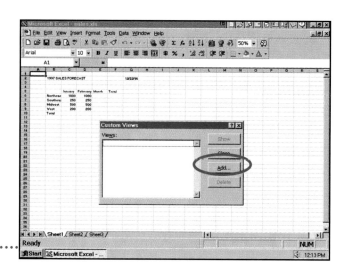

4 To save a customized view, open the **View** menu and click **Custom Views**. In the Custom Views dialog box, click the **Add** button to open the Add View dialog box.

5 Type **smallwks** and click **OK**. This names and saves the spreadsheet with the current view settings. Then click **100%** in the Zoom Control box to restore the worksheet to 100%.

6 To return to a custom view you've saved, open the **View** menu and click **Custom Views**. Double-click **smallwks** in the Views list. Excel displays the custom spreadsheet view.

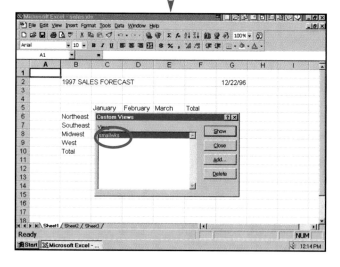

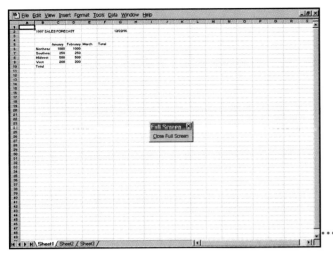

7 Open the **View** menu and click **Full Screen**. Excel displays the worksheet without the title bar, toolbars, Formula bar, and status bar. This enables you to see the full screen display of your worksheet with only the menu bar and scroll bars.

8 Click the **Close Full Screen** button on the Full Screen toolbar, located in the middle of the worksheet. Excel redisplays the title bar, toolbars, and status bar. Select **100**% from the Zoom Control box to restore the worksheet to 100%. ■

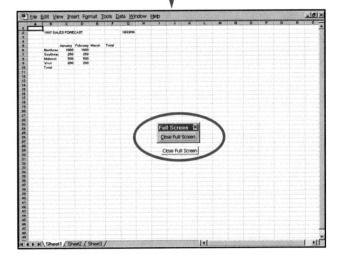

Creating and Printing a Chart

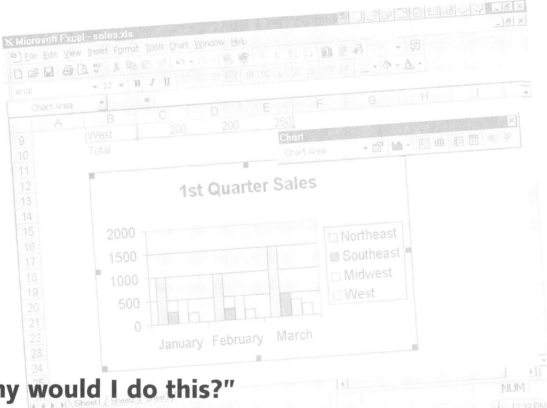

"Why would I do this?"

The easiest way to create a chart in Excel is to use the Chart Wizard feature. The Chart Wizard leads you step by step through the tasks for creating an embedded chart. Excel plots the data and creates the embedded chart where you specify on the worksheet.

You can print an embedded chart with its worksheet as you would any worksheet. For example, you might want to print the chart and worksheet together for a presentation. That way, your audience can easily see trends in a series of values.

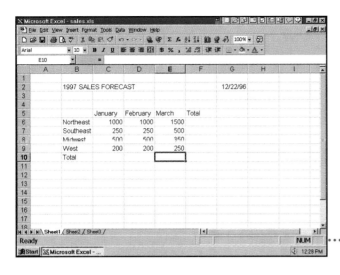

1 Change the data in the worksheet to what is shown in this figure. When you finish, your computer screen should match the one shown here.

2 Select cells **B5** to **E9** to select the range you want to chart (B5:E9).

Missing Link

Remember, you *must* select data before you can create a chart.

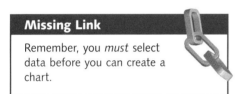

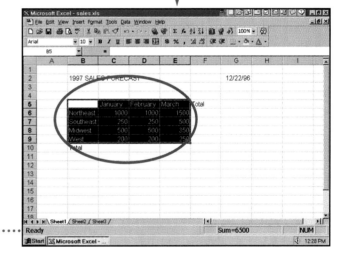

3 Click the **Chart Wizard** button on the Standard toolbar. The Chart Wizard - Step 1 of 4 dialog box appears, displaying the available chart types. The clustered column chart is the default chart type.

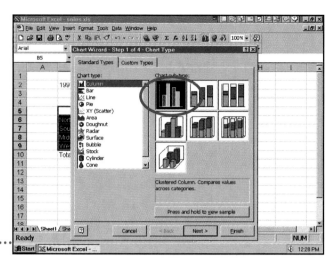

4 Select or confirm the type of chart you want—in this case, the clustered column chart.

5 Click **Next**, and Excel displays the Chart Wizard - Step 2 of 4 dialog box with a sample chart. Notice that the data series is charted in columns. As you can see, each bar represents the values for one month by territory. You want Excel to use the data series in rows so that each bar will represent the values for one item by month.

6 Click the **Rows** option button to change the plot order to show the data series in rows. Excel redisplays the chart with January, February, and March as the category (X) axis labels. The territory names now appear in the legend for the data series.

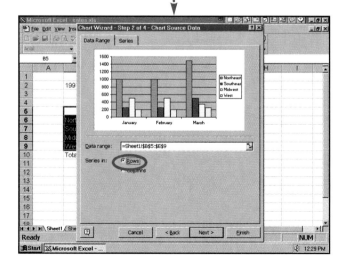

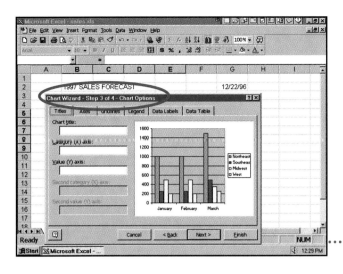

7 Click the **Next** button, and Excel displays the final dialog box, Chart Wizard - Step 3 of 4. It shows the sample chart again and gives you options for adding a legend and titles. Keep the legend that explains the data series, and add a chart title. (Or, if you want to delete the legend, choose **None**.)

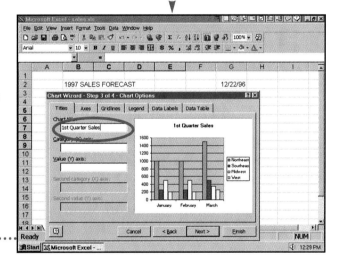

8 Click the **Chart Title** text box or press the **Tab** key. Then type **1st Quarter Sales** as the title for the chart. This gives the chart a name, so Excel redisplays the chart with the title at the top.

9 Click the **Next** button, and Excel displays the final dialog box. The Chart Wizard - Step 4 of 4 dialog box contains options for placing the chart on a separate sheet or as an object on a worksheet. Click the **As Object In** option button and select a worksheet, such as **Sheet1**.

10 Click the **Finish** button. Excel creates the new chart and displays the Chart toolbar above and to the right of the chart. Click the **Save** button on the Standard toolbar and save the file.

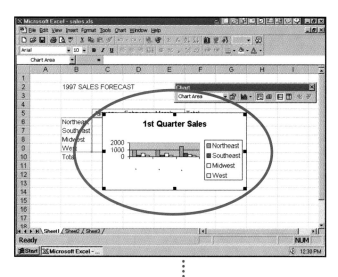

Missing Link

If you change any data in the specified chart range, Excel will update the chart accordingly to reflect the new data in the worksheet.

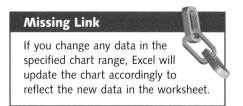

11 To drag the chart below the worksheet, drag the middle selection handle downward to make the chart taller. Now you can see the x-axis category labels. Click any cell to deselect the chart.

Puzzled?

You can stop the process of creating an embedded chart by clicking the **Cancel** button in any Chart Wizard dialog box.

12 To preview your worksheet, click the **Print Preview** button on the Standard toolbar. Then click the **Print** button on the Print Preview toolbar. In the Page Range area, click the **Page(s)** option button and type **1** in both the **From** box and **To** boxes. Then click **OK** to print the worksheet and the chart. ▪

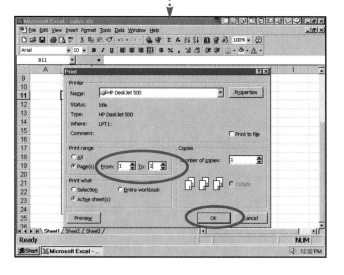

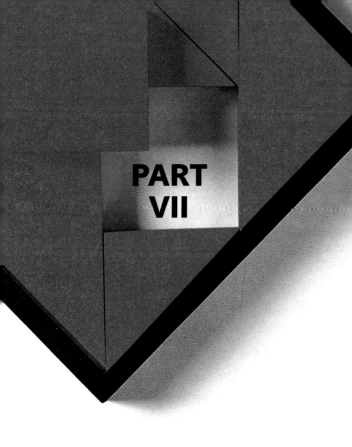

PART VII

Working with Formulas

▲ ● ■ ▲ ● ■ ▲ ●

N PART 6, "ENTERING AND EDITING DATA IN EXCEL," you learned how to enter data and change your worksheet data using various editing techniques. This section shows you how to create a formula, total cells with the SUM function, and copy a formula.

Formulas calculate a value based on the values in other cells of the worksheet. Once you enter a formula, you can change the values in the referenced cells, and Excel automatically recalculates its value based on the cell changes. You can include any cells in your formula. The cells do not have to be next to each other. Also, you can combine mathematical operations—for example, C3+C4–D5.

Functions are abbreviated formulas that perform a specific operation on a group of values. Excel provides more than 250 functions that can help you with tasks ranging from determining loan payments to calculating investment returns.

The SUM function is a shortcut for entering an addition formula. SUM is the name of the function that automatically sums entries in a range. You enter the range within parentheses. For example, first you type **=SUM(**. You can type the function in lower- or uppercase letters. Then you select the range. A dashed border called a marquee surrounds the selected range. Finally, you end the function with a parenthesis. Typing **)** tells Excel that you are finished selecting the range. Excel inserts the range coordinates in the parentheses. Alternatively, you can type **Alt+=** to create a SUM formula. This section shows you how to use the AutoSum button on the Standard toolbar to create a sum formula.

Excel's Copy command lets you copy formulas and place them in the appropriate cells. You do not have to go to each cell and enter the same formula. You also can copy one cell to another cell, and you can copy one cell to a range of cells. You learn how to use the Copy and Paste buttons to copy a formula. You also use the fill handle to copy a formula to a range of cells.

In Excel, there are three types of cell references—relative, absolute, and mixed. The type of cell reference you use in a formula determines how the formula is affected when you copy the formula into a different cell. The formulas you create in this section contain *relative cell references*. This means that when you copy a formula from one cell to another, the cell references in the formula change to reflect the cells relative to the new location of the formula.

An *absolute cell reference* is an entry in a formula that does not refer to a new cell when the formula is copied to a new cell. There are certain formulas you might want to create in which you want an entry to always refer to one specific cell value. For example, you might want to calculate the interest on several different principal amounts. The interest percentage remains unchanged, or absolute, so the entry in the formula that refers to the interest percentage is designated as an absolute cell reference. The principal amounts change, so they have relative cell reference entries in the formula. When you copy this absolute formula, the interest cell reference always refers to the one cell that contains the interest percentage.

A *mixed cell reference* is a single cell entry in a formula that contains both a relative and an absolute cell reference. A mixed cell reference is helpful when you need a formula that always refers to the values in a specific column, but the values in the rows must change—or vice versa.

Formulas can be as simple or as complex as necessary to get the job done. In this section, the calculations are restricted to the more basic mathematical formulas you work with on a daily basis. The capability of entering formulas in worksheets shows you much of the power and convenience of programs like Excel.

Adding Data with a Formula

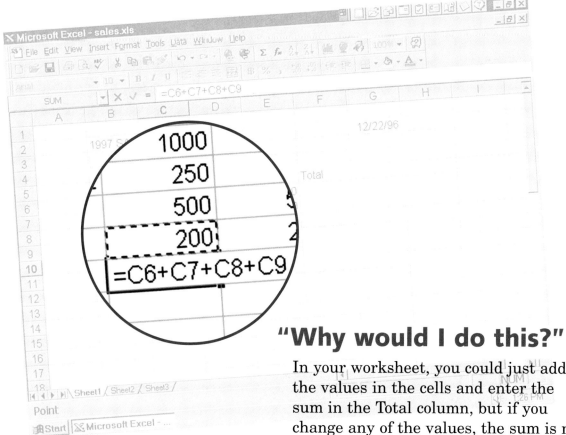

"Why would I do this?"

In your worksheet, you could just add the values in the cells and enter the sum in the Total column, but if you change any of the values, the sum is not current. Because a formula references the cells and not the values, Excel updates the sum whenever you change the values in the cells. In an expense report, you might want to enter a formula to sum your expenses. You also can use the SUM function to add values.

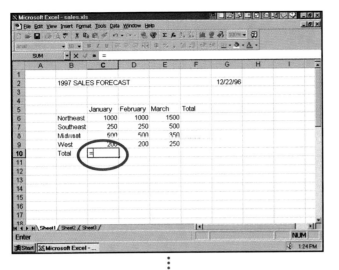

1 Click cell C10 to designate it as the cell in which you want to place the formula and where the result of the formula will appear. Then type **=** (equals sign).

Missing Link

Typing = tells Excel that you want to create a formula. You then select the cells you want to include in your formula.

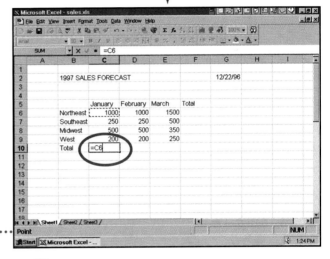

2 Click the first cell you want to include in the addition formula, such as cell C6. Excel surrounds the cell with a dashed marquee. You see =C6 in the Formula bar and in cell C10.

3 Type **+** as the operator. It tells Excel which mathematical operation you want to perform—in this case, addition. You see =C6+ in the Formula bar and in cell C10, and the cell pointer returns to C10.

Missing Link

When you create a formula, you can enter other mathematical operators: – (minus sign) for subtraction, * (asterisk) for multiplication, or / (forward slash) for division.

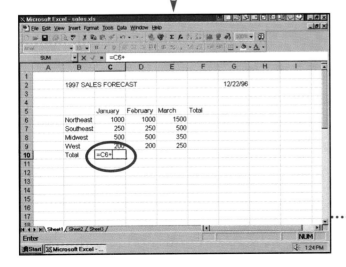

175

4 Click cell **C7**. Cell C7 is the second cell you want to include in the addition formula. A dashed marquee surrounds the cell. You see =C6+C7 in the Formula bar and in cell C10.

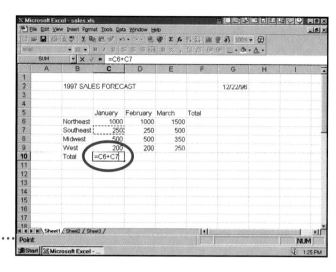

5 Type the next operator: **+**. It tells Excel which mathematical operation you want to perform—in this case, addition. You see =C6+C7+ in the Formula bar and in cell C10, and the cell pointer returns to C10.

6 Select the next cell you want to include in the addition formula: **C8**. A dashed marquee surrounds the cell. You see =C6+C7+C8 in the Formula bar and in cell C10.

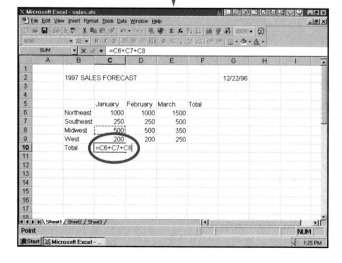

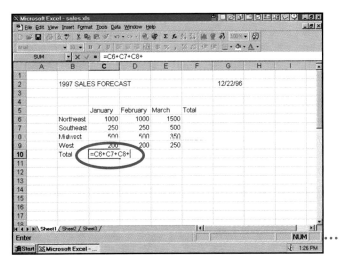

7 Type **+** as the next operator to tell Excel which mathematical operation you want to perform (addition). You see =C6+C7+C8+ in the Formula bar and in cell C10, and the cell pointer returns to cell C10.

8 Select cell **C9** as the last cell you want to include in the addition formula. A dashed marquee surrounds the cell. You see =C6+C7+C8+C9 in the Formula bar and in cell C10.

Puzzled?

To delete the most recent entry, click the **Undo** button in the Standard toolbar immediately after entering the addition formula.

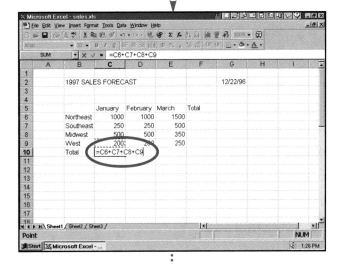

9 Press **Enter** to indicate that you are finished creating the formula. You see the result of the formula (1950) in cell C10. Whenever C10 is the active cell, the formula =C6+C7+C8+C9 appears in the Formula bar. ■

Missing Link

If you see number signs (#) in the cell, the entry is too long. To see the actual number, you can change the column width. See Task 50, "Changing Column Width."

46

Totaling Cells with the SUM Function

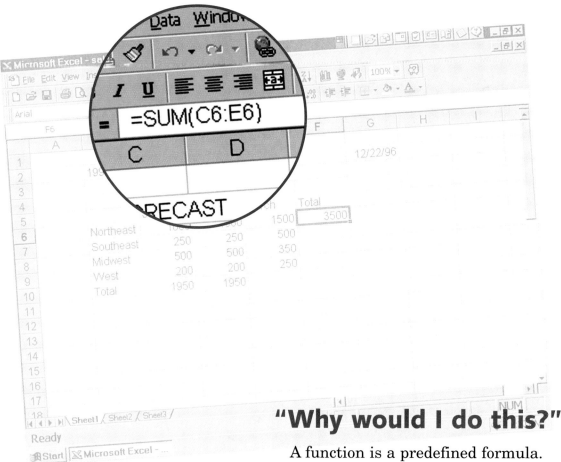

"Why would I do this?"

A function is a predefined formula. You provide the variable parts of the formula, and Excel calculates the result. The SUM function enables you to sum a range. If you later insert or delete rows (or columns), Excel automatically updates the total. For example, you can replace a lengthy column or row total formula with a simple SUM function.

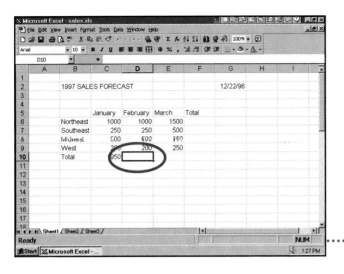

1 Select the cell where you want to place the SUM function. Click cell **D10**.

2 Double-click the **AutoSum** button (the button that contains the Greek Sigma symbol) on the Standard toolbar. This enters the SUM function in the Formula bar and in the cell. As you can see here, =SUM(D6:D9) appears in the Formula bar. You see the result of the formula, 1950, in cell D10.

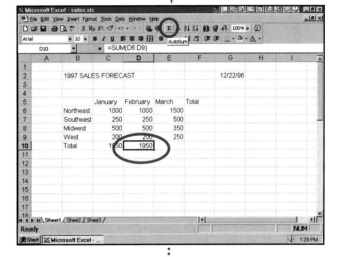

Puzzled?

If you click the AutoSum button once and you see the formula in the cell and in the Formula bar, click the AutoSum button again.

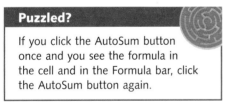

3 Click cell **F6**. Then enter the SUM function in cell E5 (click the AutoSum button). The formula =SUM(C6:E6) appears in the Formula bar, and you see the result of the formula, 3500, in cell F6. ∎

Missing Link

You can also type =**SUM(**, click and drag the cells you want to include in the SUM function, and then press **Enter**. Excel inserts the closing parenthesis in the SUM formula.

Copying a Formula

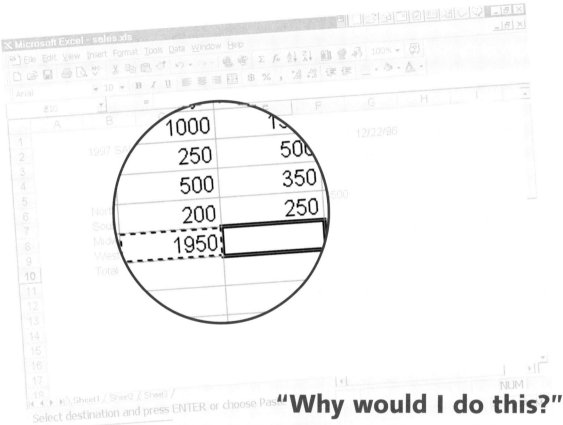

"Why would I do this?"

When you build your worksheet, you often use the same data and formulas in more than one cell. With Excel's Copy command, you can create the initial data or formula once, and then place copies of this information in the appropriate cells. You do not have to go to each cell and enter the same data. For example, you may want to copy a formula across a totals row. That way you wouldn't have to type each formula to add up the row of numbers.

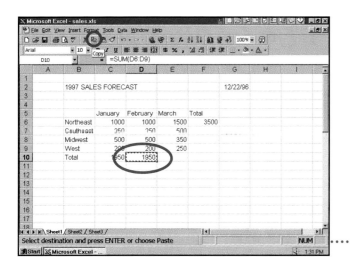

1 Click cell **D10**, which contains the formula you want to copy. Then click the **Copy** button on the Standard toolbar. A dashed marquee surrounds the cell you are copying, and the message Select destination and press ENTER or choose Paste appears in the status bar to remind you to complete the task.

2 Select the cell in which you want to place the copy. For example, click cell **E10**.

Missing Link

The copied formula references the current column by *relative addressing*. With relative addressing, Excel automatically adjusts the cell references in the copied formula to reflect the cells relative to the new location.

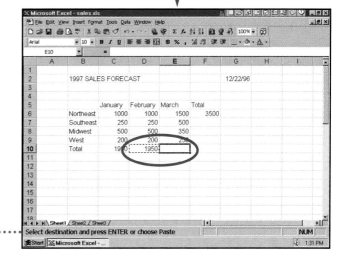

3 Click the **Paste** button on the Standard toolbar, and Excel pastes a copy of the data into the cells. The result of the formula appears in cell E10, and the Formula bar shows =SUM(E6:E9).

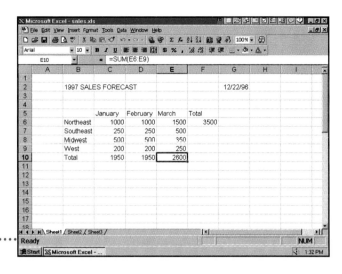

4 Press **Esc** to remove the copy marquee.

> **Puzzled?**
>
> If you delete values used in for-
> mulas throughout the worksheet,
> those formulas will return errors.

5 Click cell **F6**. Then drag the fill handle
downward across cells **F7–F10**. This copies
the formula in cell F6 into cells F7, F8, F9,
and F10. When you finish, save the file. ■

> **Missing Link**
>
> You can make a cell reference
> partially absolute so that either
> the row or column portion of the
> reference will adjust. A dollar sign pre-
> ceding the row portion of the refer-
> ence makes the row absolute; a dollar
> sign preceding the column portion
> makes the column absolute. To enter
> an absolute cell reference in a for-
> mula, press **F4** until you see the
> absolute reference you want.

PART VIII

Formatting the Worksheet

FORMATTING THE WORKSHEET means you can change the appearance of data on your worksheet. With Excel's formatting tools, you can make your worksheet more attractive and readable.

You can align data in a cell left, center, or right. The default alignment is General. *General alignment* means that numbers are right-aligned and text is left-aligned.

Numeric values are usually more than just numbers. They represent a dollar value, a date, a percent, or some other value. You can select the format type that appears as a real value in the Format Cells dialog box. To narrow the list of formats, first select a category in the Category list. Then specify the number of decimal places. The default number of decimal places is two.

If you want to reset the column width to the original setting, choose the **Format Column**, **Standard Width** command and click **OK** in the Standard Width dialog box.

A *font* is a style of type that is a particular typeface and size. Excel displays various fonts and font sizes in the Formatting toolbar. You can use the fonts provided by Excel as well as fonts designed especially for your printer. If Excel does not have a screen version of the printer font you select, it substitutes a font. In this case, the printout looks different than the screen.

In Excel, you can print your worksheets using a basic printing procedure or you can enhance the printout using several print options. It is fairly simple to print a worksheet in Excel.

First you set up the format for your printout. You can insert manual page breaks in your worksheet to split the worksheet on two or more pages. Otherwise, Excel automatically sets the page breaks. There are three ways to set page breaks:

- At the right side of each page, letting Excel break the pages at the bottom automatically.

- At the bottom of each page, letting Excel break the pages on the right side automatically.

- At the bottom and right sides of a page, which is the manual page break option.

Page breaks remain on the worksheet until you remove them. Establishing new page breaks does not change existing page breaks. It just adds to them. Page Break Preview enables you to view and change page breaks, making it easier to paginate spreadsheets.

If the worksheet is still too large to print on one page, you can change the top, bottom, left, and right margins. You also might consider reducing the printout using the Adjust To option in the Page Setup dialog box. Some printers will let you reduce or enlarge the printout as it prints. Although 100% is normal size, you can enter the desired reduction or enlargement percentage you want.

The Fit To option prints the worksheet at full size to fit the size of the page. You can enter the number of pages in the Page(s) Wide By and the Tall text boxes to specify the document's width and height. This option may not be available on all printers.

It is a good idea to save your worksheets before printing— just in case a printer error or other problem occurs. You won't lose any work since the last time you saved the worksheet. You learn how to print your worksheet from the Page Setup dialog box. But if you already set up your print options and you're back to the worksheet, you can just click the **Print** button on the Standard toolbar to print your worksheet.

Aligning Data

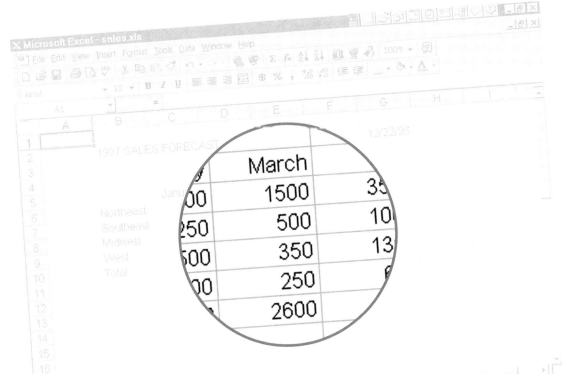

"Why would I do this?"

When you enter data into a cell, numbers, dates, and times automatically align with the right side of the cell. Text aligns with the left side of the cell. You can change the alignment of information at any time. For instance, you may want to fine-tune the appearance of column headings across columns, or you can right-align column headings across the columns to line up the headings with the numbers that are right-aligned.

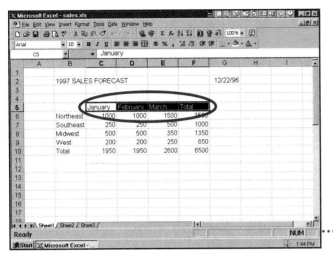

1 In your SALES.XLS worksheet, hold down the mouse button and drag over cells **C5**, **D5**, **E5**, and **F5**. This selects the range you want to right-align: C5:F5. Notice that these entries are left-aligned.

2 Click the **Align Right** button on the Formatting toolbar, and Excel right-aligns the contents of each cell in the range. Click any cell to deselect the range. ■

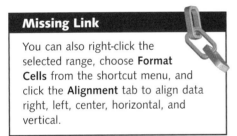

Missing Link

You can also right-click the selected range, choose **Format Cells** from the shortcut menu, and click the **Alignment** tab to align data right, left, center, horizontal, and vertical.

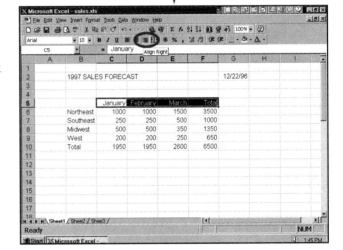

189

TASK

49

Displaying Dollar Signs, Commas, and Decimal Places

"Why would I do this?"

Excel enables you to display numeric values in many ways. *Formatting* a number means changing the way it is displayed. You can format the number 500 to look like currency, in which case it's displayed as $500.00. You can even specify as many decimal places as you want to display.

You can choose from four currency styles. The first choice is Currency with negative numbers preceded by a minus sign. The second choice is Currency with negative numbers that appear in the color red. The third choice is Currency with negative numbers enclosed in parentheses. The fourth choice is Currency with negative numbers enclosed in parentheses and appear in the color red.

	Total
$	3,500
$	1,000
$	1,350
$	650
$	6,500

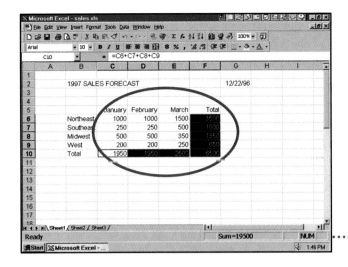

1 Hold down the mouse button and drag the mouse to select cells **F6** to **F10**. Then hold down the **Ctrl** key and select cells **C10** to **E10**. This selects the ranges F6:F10 and C10:E10, in which you want to display dollar signs.

2 Click the **Currency Style** button on the Formatting toolbar, and then click any cell to deselect the range. Excel automatically applies Currency style, displaying dollar signs, commas, and two decimal places.

Puzzled?

If any cell displays number signs, you can widen the column to display the numbers. Double-click the line to the right of the column letter for the column you want to adjust.

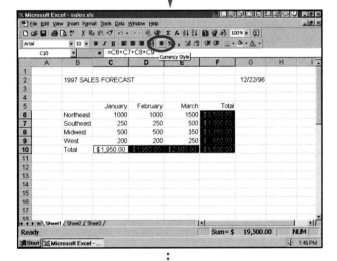

3 Hold down the mouse button and drag the mouse to select cells **C6** to **E9**. This selects the range C6:E9 in which you want to display commas.

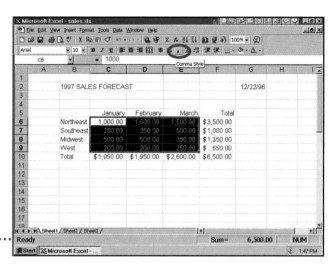

4 Click the **Comma Style** button on the Formatting toolbar. As you can see here, Excel displays commas and two decimal places in the selected cells.

5 Click the **Decrease Decimal** button on the Formatting toolbar, and Excel moves the decimal point one place to the right. Note that the number of decimal places for the numbers in cells C6 to E9 has changed from two to one.

6 Click the **Decrease Decimal** button on the Formatting toolbar again, and then click any cell to deselect the range. As you can see, the number of decimal places for the numbers in cells C6 to E9 is now zero.

Missing Link

If you select zero decimal places, Excel rounds the values to fit this format. For example, if you enter 7.5 in a cell, Excel rounds this number to 8 when formatting to zero decimal places.

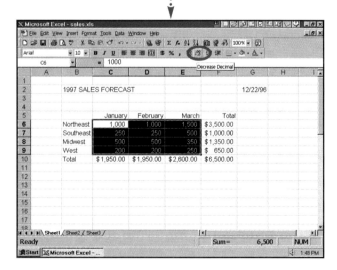

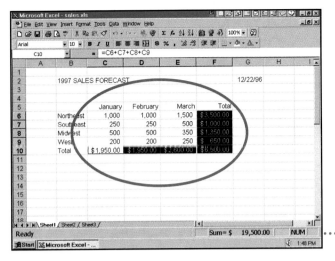

7 Select cells **F6** through **F10** and cells **C10** through **E10** so you can format them to display zero decimal places.

8 Repeat steps 5 and 6 to specify zero decimal places for the numbers in the selected ranges, and then click any cell to deselect the ranges. The number of decimal places for the numbers in cells F6 through F10 and C10 through E10 has changed from two to zero decimal places. ■

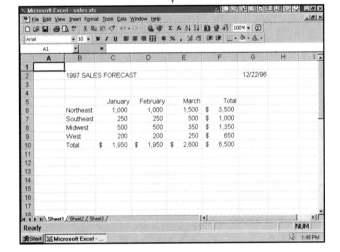

Puzzled?

To undo the most recent formatting change, click the **Undo** button on the Standard toolbar.

Changing Column Width

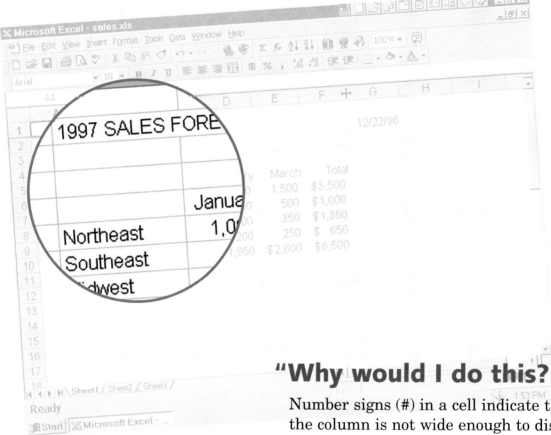

"Why would I do this?"

Number signs (#) in a cell indicate that the column is not wide enough to display the numeric value or the results of the formula contained in the cell. Often, the formatting (and the selected font) makes the entry longer than the default column width. Text that does not fit is not cut off, it's just not visible. However, the entire text entry appears in the Formula bar.

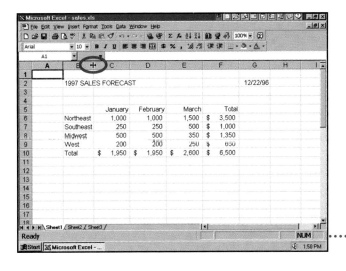

1 Position the mouse pointer on the line to the right of the column you want to adjust—in this case, to the right of column letter B. The mouse pointer changes to a double-arrow.

2 Press and hold the mouse button, and drag to make the column the correct width. When it's wide enough to display the longest entry, release the mouse button. Excel widens the column.

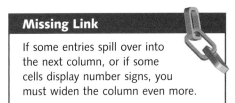

Missing Link

If some entries spill over into the next column, or if some cells display number signs, you must widen the column even more.

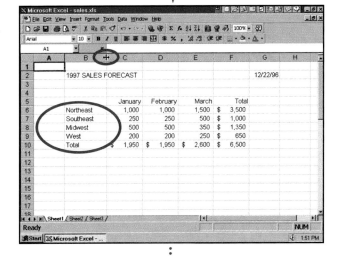

3 As a result of your change in step 2, the columns are now different widths. If you want all columns to have the same widths, use the AutoFit feature. Double-click the line to the right of the column letter for the column you want to adjust: column C. Excel's AutoFit feature automatically adjusts the width of the column based on the column's longest entry. Repeat this step for columns D, E, and F. ■

TASK

Inserting and Removing Page Breaks

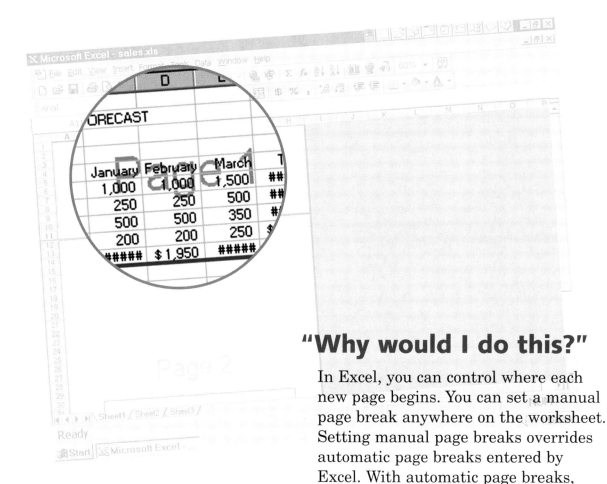

"Why would I do this?"

In Excel, you can control where each new page begins. You can set a manual page break anywhere on the worksheet. Setting manual page breaks overrides automatic page breaks entered by Excel. With automatic page breaks, Excel decides where page breaks will appear in the worksheet based on the standard paper size selected in the Page Setup dialog box.

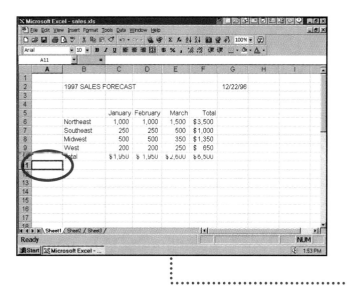

1 Select the cell below where you want to insert a page break. For this example, click cell **A11**. After you insert the page break, Excel will print everything above row 11 on one page and then start a new page.

Missing Link

If you click a cell that is not in the far left column of the work-sheet and then you select the Insert Page Break command, Excel inserts manual page breaks above and to the left of the selected cell.

2 Open the **Insert** menu and choose **Page Break**. The manual page break appears above the row containing the active cell.

Missing Link

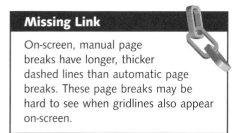

On-screen, manual page breaks have longer, thicker dashed lines than automatic page breaks. These page breaks may be hard to see when gridlines also appear on-screen.

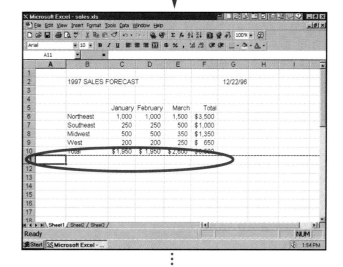

3 Open the **View** menu and choose **Page Break Preview** to preview the page breaks in the worksheet. The Welcome to Page Break Preview dialog box appears.

4 Click **OK** to clear the Welcome to Page Break Preview box from the screen.

> **Puzzled?**
>
> If you insert the page break in the wrong place, click the **Undo** button on the Standard toolbar immediately. Or, just select the cell immediately below and to the right of the page break line(s) and choose **Insert, Remove Page Break**.

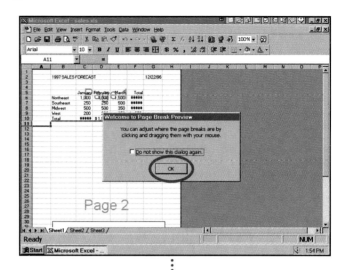

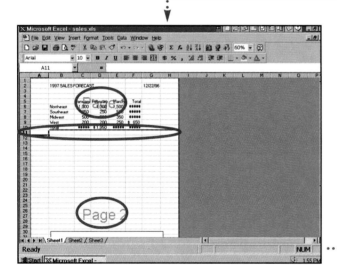

5 You see a preview of how page breaks on your worksheet will look when you print it. Notice that the manual page break is a solid line above row 11; Page 1 is displayed across the first page, and Page 2 is displayed across the second page.

6 To return to Normal View, open the **View** menu and choose **Normal**. ■

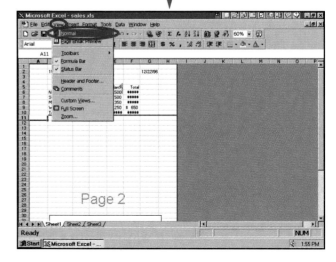

Selecting a Print Area and Printing Column and Row Headings

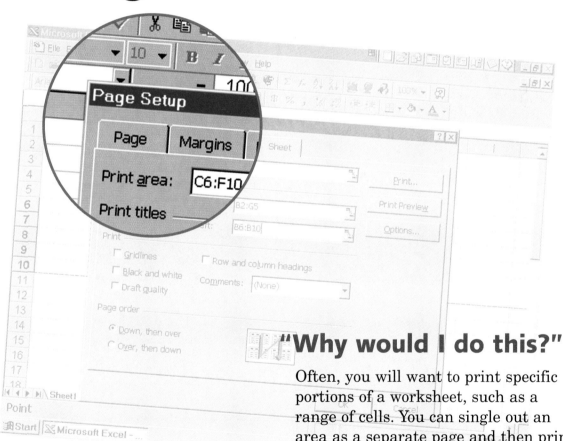

"Why would I do this?"

Often, you will want to print specific portions of a worksheet, such as a range of cells. You can single out an area as a separate page and then print that page. You can also select titles that are located on the top edge and left side of your worksheet and print them on every page of the printout.

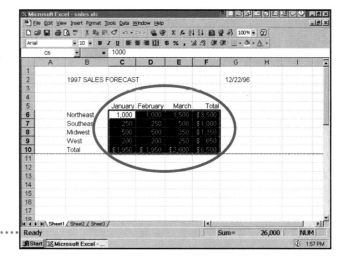

1 Select the range **C6:F10**. This specifies the range C6:F10 as the print area.

Missing Link

Do not include the title, subtitle, or column and row titles in the print area. If you include these titles in the print area, Excel will print the titles twice.

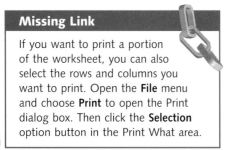

2 Open the **File** menu, choose **Print Area**, and then click **Set Print Area**. The automatic page breaks appear to the left and right and the top and bottom of the range C6:F10. Notice that the automatic page breaks override the manual page break; the manual page break no longer appears above row 11.

Puzzled?

To remove the print area, open the **File** menu, choose **Print Area**, and click **Clear Print Area**.

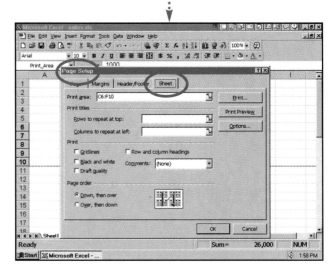

3 Open the **File** menu and choose **Page Setup**. Excel displays the Page Setup dialog box. Click the **Sheet** tab to display the Sheet options.

Missing Link

If you want to print a portion of the worksheet, you can also select the rows and columns you want to print. Open the **File** menu and choose **Print** to open the Print dialog box. Then click the **Selection** option button in the Print What area.

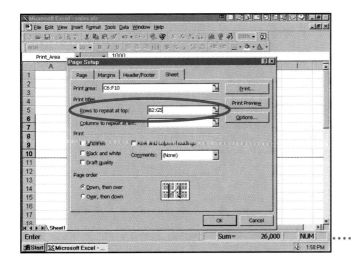

4 Click in the **Rows to Repeat at Top** text box or press **Tab** twice to move the insertion point there. Type **B2:G5** to specify the range you want to repeat at the top of every page.

5 Click in the **Columns to Repeat at Left** text box or press **Tab** to move the insertion point there. Type **B6:B10** to specify the range you want to repeat at the left side of every page.

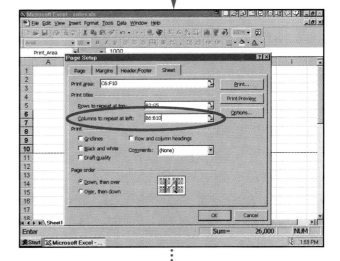

Missing Link

To change the page orientation, click the **Page** tab in the Page Setup dialog box, and then choose **Portrait** or **Landscape**.

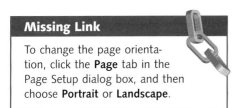

6 Click **OK** to confirm your choices. Excel displays a dashed line border around the print area. All data above and to the left of the dashed line border will repeat on every page. ■

Puzzled?

To remove the rows and columns you want to repeat, delete the cell coordinates in the Rows to Repeat at Top and Columns to Repeat at Left text boxes.

Adding Headers and Footers

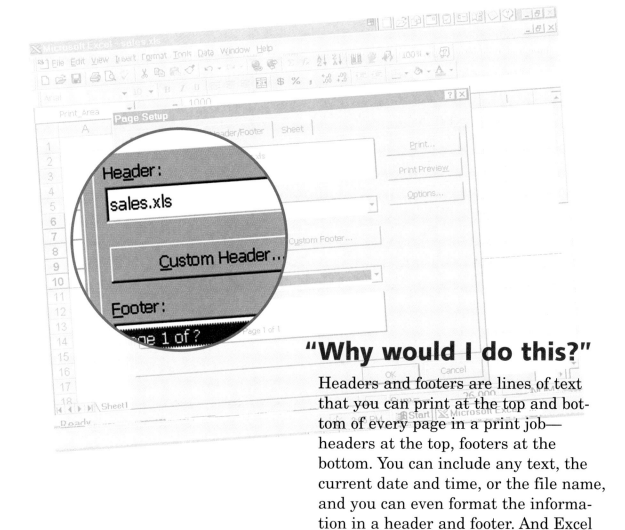

"Why would I do this?"

Headers and footers are lines of text that you can print at the top and bottom of every page in a print job— headers at the top, footers at the bottom. You can include any text, the current date and time, or the file name, and you can even format the information in a header and footer. And Excel gives you a variety of built-in headers and footers to choose from in case you don't want to create your own.

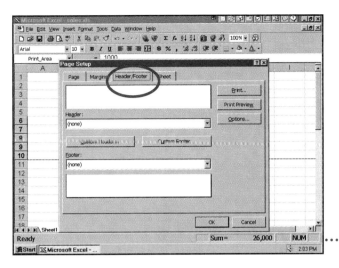

1 Open the **File** menu and click **Page Setup**. Excel opens the Page Setup dialog box. In the dialog box, click the **Header/Footer** tab to see the header and footer options. The default header is (none).

2 Click the **Header** drop-down arrow, and a list of suggested header information appears. Scroll through the list to **sales.xls**, and then click it. The sample header appears centered at the top of the box.

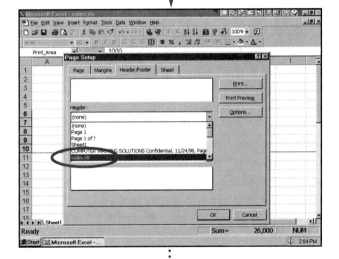

Puzzled?

If something unexpected prints at the top or bottom of your worksheet, check the Header or Footer text box. If you don't want a header or footer, choose **None** in the Header or Footer suggestions list.

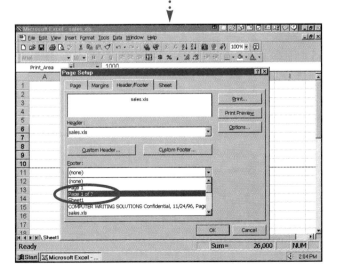

3 By default, the footer "(none)" appears in the Footer text box. Click the **Footer** drop-down arrow, and a list of suggested footer information appears. Scroll through the list to **Page 1 of ?**, and then click it. The sample footer appears centered at the bottom of the box. Click **OK**. ■

Missing Link

If you want to customize a header or footer, click the **Custom Header** or **Custom Footer** button and enter the information you want in the Left, Center, and Right sections.

Previewing and Printing the Worksheet

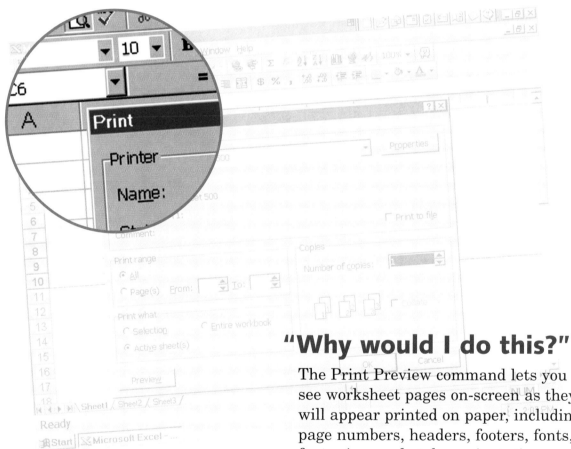

"Why would I do this?"

The Print Preview command lets you see worksheet pages on-screen as they will appear printed on paper, including page numbers, headers, footers, fonts, fonts sizes and styles, orientation, and margins. Previewing your worksheet is a great way to catch formatting errors, such as incorrect margins and over-lapped data. Excel gives you many print options for customizing the way you print your worksheets.

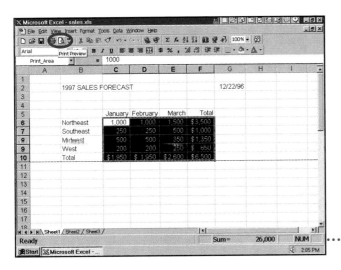

1 Click the **Print Preview** button on the Standard toolbar (it's a shortcut for selecting the Print Preview command). You see a preview of how your worksheet will look when you print it.

2 Click the **Zoom** button at the top of the screen to enlarge the preview to its actual size. This enables you to examine the printout more closely.

Missing Link

To preview the worksheet, your monitor must have graphics capability. If you see an error message, your monitor probably cannot display the worksheet. You must print the worksheet to see how it looks after step 1.

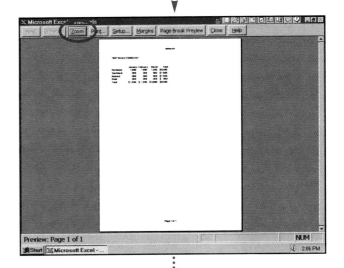

3 Click the **Print** button on the Print Preview toolbar, and Excel displays the Print dialog box.

4 The name of your printer appears at the top of the dialog box. Make any necessary changes to the print options.

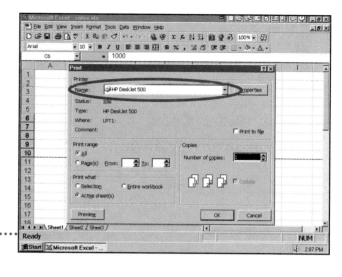

Missing Link

When you installed Windows, you also installed the printer. If no printer is installed, refer to the Windows manual.

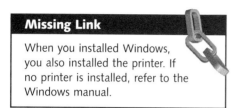

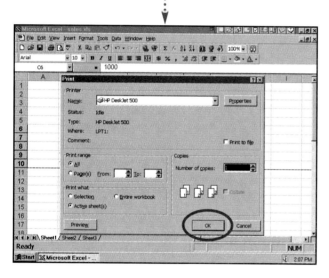

5 Click **OK** to start the print job. ■

Puzzled?

During a print job, Excel displays a dialog box on-screen. To stop the print job, double-click the Printer icon on the Windows taskbar to display the printer queue dialog box. Then click the document name, open the **Document** menu, and click **Cancel Printing** to cancel the print job. Click the **Close** (X) button to close the dialog box.

PART IX

Building and Managing a Presentation in PowerPoint

N POWERPOINT, YOU CREATE YOUR PRESENTATION using just one file. It contains everything you need—an outline of your presentation, your slides, audience handouts, and even your speaker's notes.

You can use PowerPoint to plan every aspect of a winning presentation. PowerPoint even helps you organize the ideas in your presentation. To get this help, use PowerPoint's AutoContent Wizard. This wizard quickly creates your presentation, including a title slide and several slides containing bulleted lists.

The wizard gives you ideas on how to organize your presentation, too. When you use the wizard, you choose from six professionally designed ways of organizing your presentation. All you need to do is type your own ideas in place of the suggestions the wizard provides. With AutoContent Wizard, you have a professional communications consultant helping you with each step!

When you choose the General presentation type, your presentation begins with a slide stating the topic of discussion. You continue with a slide that lists your main ideas. Next come slides that provide details on each subtopic, followed by slides that provide examples. You conclude with a summary and a statement of the next step that should be taken. You can set up your General presentation in the following ways:

- *Selling a Product or Idea*: You start with your objective, and continue by stating the customer's requirements, the features of your product, your competitive strengths, the key benefits you can provide, and the customer's next steps.

- *Training*: You start by stating the subject and agenda. You continue with slides that provide an overview and define your vocabulary. Next are slides for each topic you want to cover. You conclude with a summary and a list of other information sources.

- *Reporting Progress*: You begin by providing background, and then you specify the status at present. You continue with slides that state the accomplishments thus far, the schedule, the issues that have arisen, and your prioritization of the issues. You conclude by discussing the next phase.

- *Recommending a Strategy*: You begin by stating your objective in the presentation, and continue with the present situation, the desired outcome, the potential strategies, the advantages and disadvantages of your proposed strategy, and your recommendation.

- *Communicating Bad News*: You start by providing some background on the situation. Next you consider the alternatives. You then provide a recommendation and a vision for the future. You conclude by specifying a time frame for the expected results.

AutoContent Wizard creates your presentation with a series of bulleted list slides. These contain lines of text preceded by a bullet. For an effective presentation, you should vary your slides by adding new objects or components that can be combined to create various layouts. For example, you might add clip art pictures, a table, a chart, or an organization chart to create visual interest and stimulation.

When you finish creating your slides, you can type speaker's notes and preview your presentation. You then save your presentation—your outline, slides, and notes—in just one presentation file, which you can easily open later and fine-tune the way you want.

With PowerPoint, you can print your outline, speaker's notes, and audience handouts on paper. For a more professional-looking presentation, consider producing overhead transparencies, a computer slide show, or 35mm slides.

TASK

55

Creating a Presentation with AutoContent Wizard

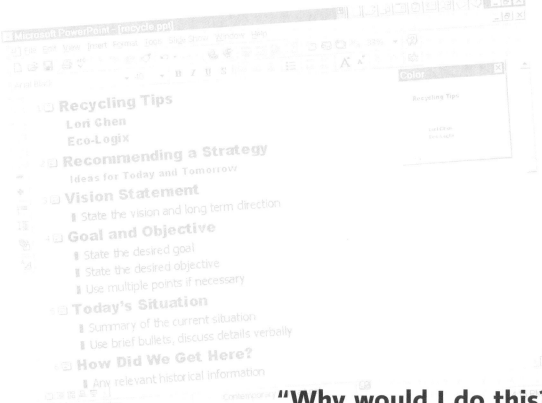

"Why would I do this?"

With PowerPoint, you could begin with a new presentation from scratch . . . but leave that to the experts. Creating a new presentation is so much easier and faster with AutoContent Wizard. It's the best way to get started with PowerPoint.

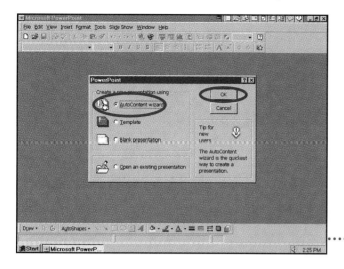

1 Start PowerPoint. (See Task 1: "Starting and Exiting Microsoft Office 97 Programs" if you need instructions.) PowerPoint opens the PowerPoint dialog box shown here. Click the **AutoContent Wizard** option button, if necessary, and then click **OK**. PowerPoint opens the first AutoContent Wizard dialog box.

2 The welcome information for AutoContent Wizard appears in this dialog box. Click the **Next** button to continue to the next step.

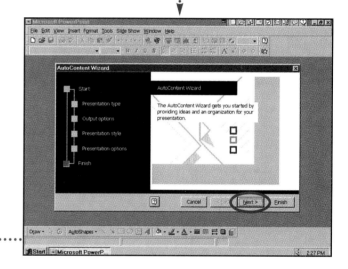

3 In the list on the left, **Presentation Type** is selected. Click the **General** button, and then select **Recommending a Strategy** from the list on the right. This specifies the presentation type and how you want the wizard to organize your ideas. Click the **Next** button, and PowerPoint brings up the next AutoContent Wizard dialog box.

4 Click **Next** to confirm the currently selected Output options. In this case, PowerPoint uses the default option: Presentations, Informal Meetings, and Handouts. PowerPoint brings up the next AutoContent Wizard dialog box.

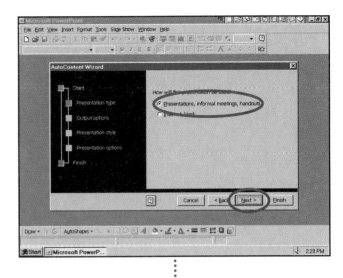

Puzzled?

You can stop the AutoContent Wizard's progress at any time by clicking **Cancel** in the AutoContent Wizard dialog box. Then start over. If you want to return to any of the dialog boxes, click the **Back** button.

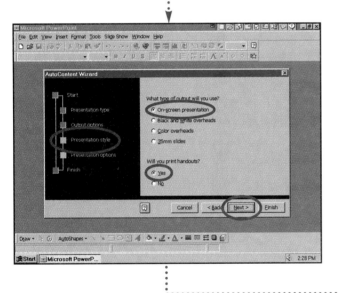

5 For the output type, choose the **On-Screen Presentation** option and choose **Yes** for handouts. Then click the **Next** button. PowerPoint brings up another AutoContent Wizard dialog box.

6 In the **Presentation Title** text box, type **Recycling Tips**. Press **Tab** to move to the Your Name text box and type **Lori Chen**. Press **Tab** again and type **Eco-Logix** in the Additional Information box. Click the **Next** button, and PowerPoint brings up another AutoContent Wizard dialog box.

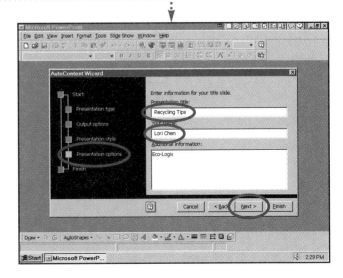

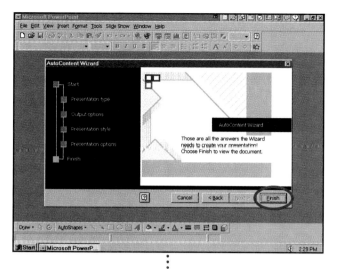

7 Click the **Finish** button. PowerPoint creates the presentation and displays an outline of the material on your slides.

Missing Link

Io change the default presentation design for the Recommending a Strategy presentation, click the **Apply Design** button on the Standard toolbar and choose a design (such as Contemporary Portrait).

8 A sample title slide and the Common Tasks toolbar appear in the presentation window. Click the **Close** (X) button on the Common Tasks toolbar to close it. Then save the file and name it RECYCLE (see Task 6, "Saving and Closing a File"). ■

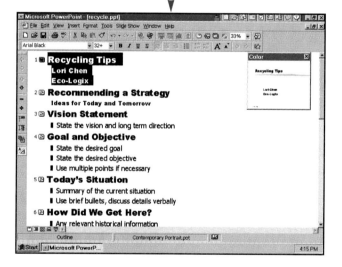

TASK

56

Using Outline View

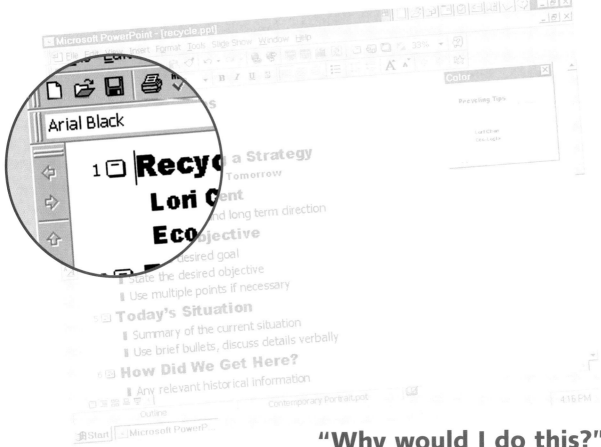

"Why would I do this?"

Outline view enables you to quickly lay out main ideas in your presentation just by typing over the wizard's suggestions.

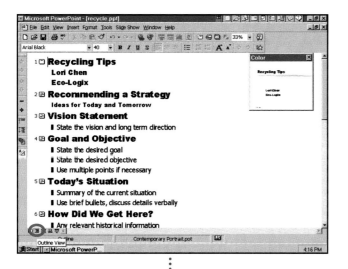

1 If necessary, click the **Outline View** button (the button that contains several horizontal lines) on the View toolbar at the bottom of the presentation window.

Missing Link

In Outline view, the Outline toolbar appears vertically along the left side of the presentation window. These tools help you work with your outline.

2 Click the **Show Formatting** button on the Outline toolbar. PowerPoint then displays your text using the fonts and font sizes the wizard selected for you. (If Show Formatting is already turned on, clicking this button turns off the feature and hides the formatting.) The formatted text looks nice, but it's easier to create your presentation when you can see more text in the window.

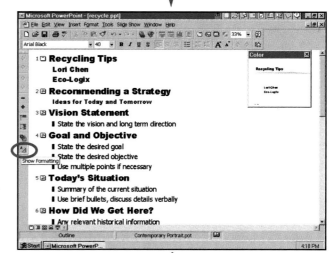

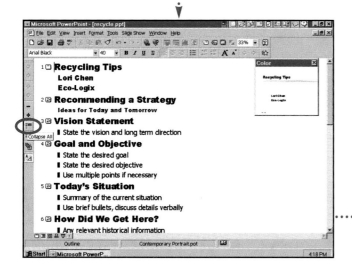

3 Click the **Collapse All** button on the Outline toolbar. Now you see only the title for each slide, and you are better able to see the overall outline of your presentation.

Missing Link

A thick gray line under a title indicates that some text is hidden.

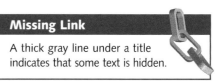

4 To select a slide in the outline, click the appropriate slide icon. For example, move the mouse pointer to the **Vision Statement** slide icon. When the mouse becomes a four-headed arrow, click the left mouse button.

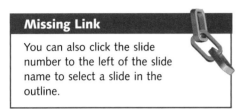

Missing Link

You can also click the slide number to the left of the slide name to select a slide in the outline.

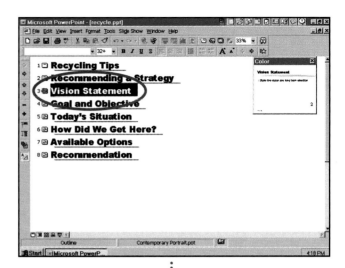

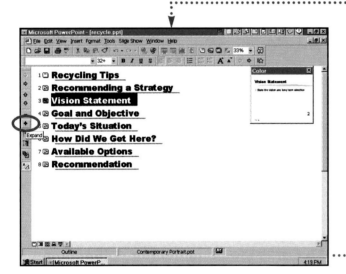

5 Click the **Expand** button on the Outline toolbar to see the text for the selected slide only.

6 Click the **Collapse** button on the Outline toolbar to hide the text on the selected slide again, so that only the title appears.

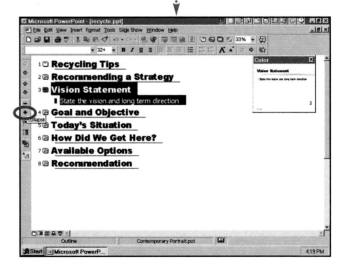

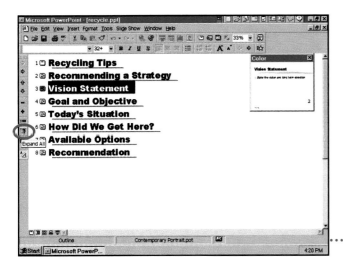

7 Click the **Expand All** button on the Outline toolbar. Your outline now displays all the main text under each title.

8 Click the down scroll arrow in the vertical scroll bar to view potions of the outline that are not currently visible in the viewing area. ■

Missing Link

You can also drag down the scroll box or press **PgDn** to see hidden portions of the outline. To scroll back up, click the up scroll arrow, drag the scroll box up, or press **PgUp**.

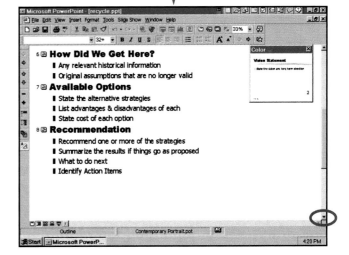

Working with Text in an Outline

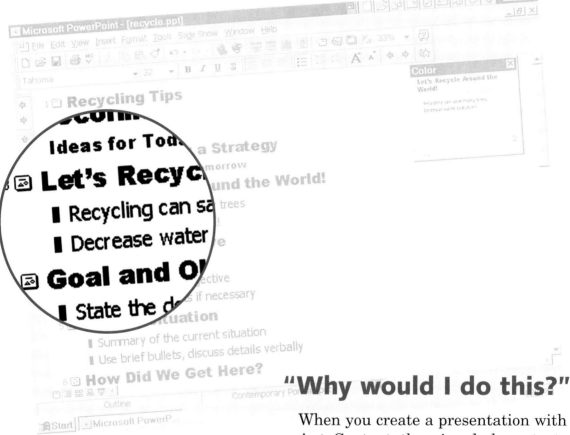

"Why would I do this?"

When you create a presentation with AutoContent, the wizard places text on each slide it creates. This text contains great tips for creating a high-impact presentation. You can change this text to express the ideas you want to convey.

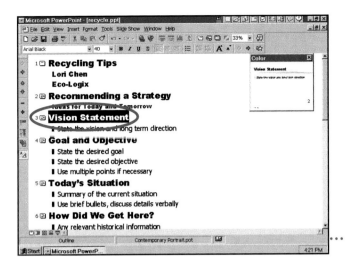

1 Select the slide name you want to change—in this case, Vision Statement. To do so, scroll to the top of the outline so the Vision Statement title is displayed. Click in front of the word "Vision" and drag the mouse to the end of the word "Statement."

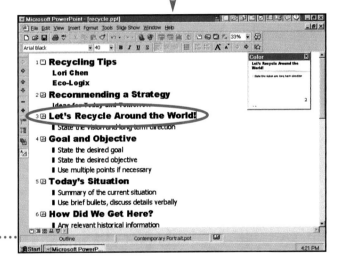

2 Type **Let's Recycle Around the World!**. As you type, the new text replaces the old text.

3 Click and drag (as in step 1) or just click the bullet next to the slide name "State the vision and long term direction." This selects the slide name you want to change. Then type **Recycling can save many trees**. As you type, the new text replaces the old text.

221

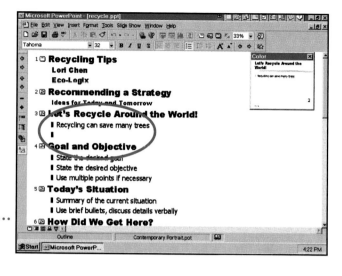

4 Press **Enter** to start a new line. PowerPoint adds a bullet to the beginning of the new line.

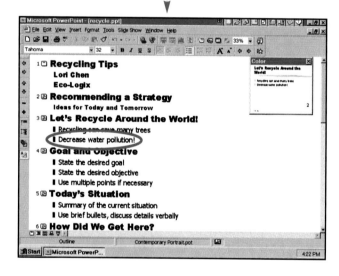

5 Type **Decrease water pollution!** as the new text for the bullet. ■

Viewing and Correcting Slides

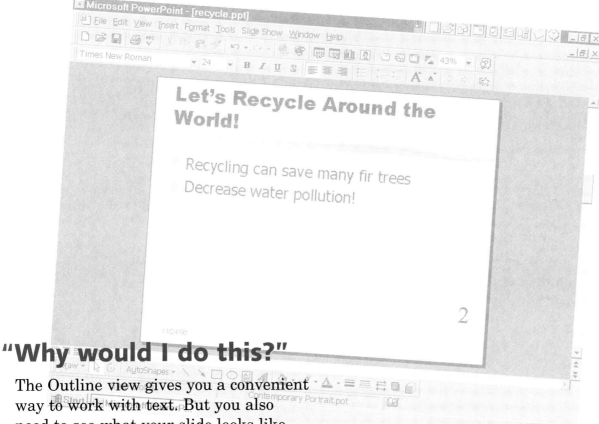

"Why would I do this?"

The Outline view gives you a convenient way to work with text. But you also need to see what your slide looks like. Perhaps you have too much text on a line in a bulleted list. Switching to the *Slide view* enables you to see how your slide will look. Outline view shows only the title and main text of the slide—it does not show graphics, such as clip art, graphs, or drawings.

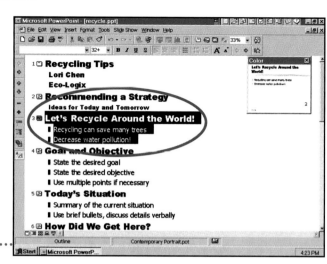

1 Select the slide you want to see in Slide View. For example, select the **Let's Recycle Around the World!** slide (see Task 57: "Working with Text in an Outline").

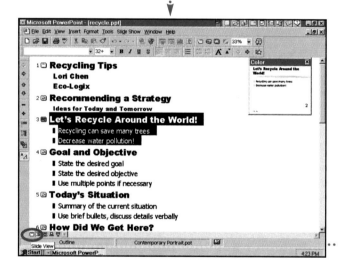

2 Click the **Slide View** button on the View toolbar to switch to Slide view. You can also double-click the slide icon or the slide title to switch to Slide view.

3 As you can see, the bulleted list slide you highlighted in the outline appears on-screen. Click the text next to the first bullet (the text you want to change). A thick bar appears around the text area; it indicates that you can edit text in Slide view.

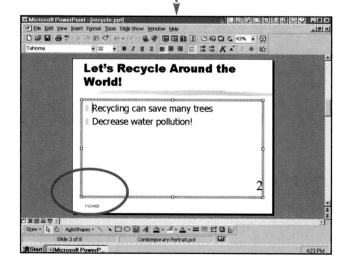

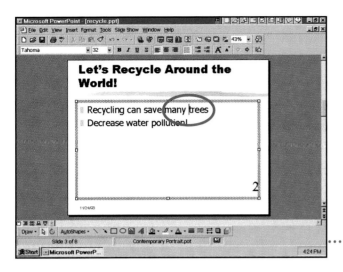

4 Move the insertion point to where you want to insert text. For this example, click before the 'T' in "Trees" in the text for the first bullet.

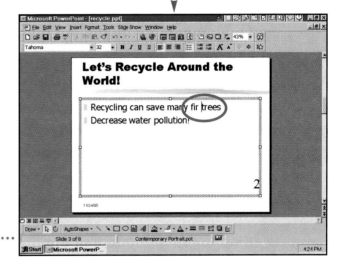

5 Type **fir** and press the **Spacebar**. This enters the new text.

6 Click the **Previous Slide** button at the bottom of the vertical scroll bar. This displays the previous slide, which is your title slide.

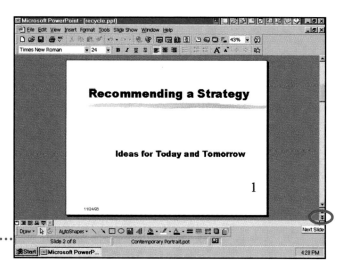

7 Click the **Next Slide** button at the bottom of the vertical scroll bar to display the next slide.

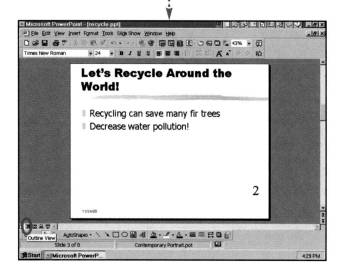

8 To switch back to Outline view, click the **Outline View** button on the View toolbar. PowerPoint switches back to Outline view and automatically updates your outline to include the changes you made in Slide view. ■

Changing the Slide Layout

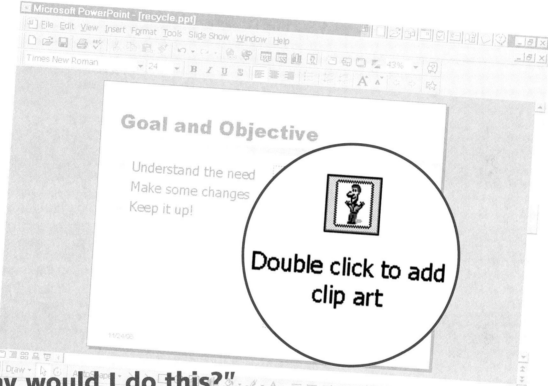

"Why would I do this?"

When the AutoContent Wizard lays out your presentation, it creates a series of bulleted list slides. However, one text slide after another makes a very boring presentation. To add visual interest to your presentation, you can vary the layout of your slides. You can choose from 21 slide layouts (called *AutoLayouts*), including many that enable you to add visually interesting features, such as clip art, tables, and graphs.

1 Select the title text **Goal and Objective** for slide 3 in the Outline view. Then type **What We Can Do** to change the slide name.

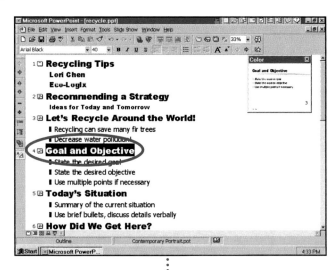

Puzzled?

If you're not in Outline view, click the **Outline View** button on the View toolbar. If the text in slide 3 is hidden, click the **Expand** tool on the Outline toolbar.

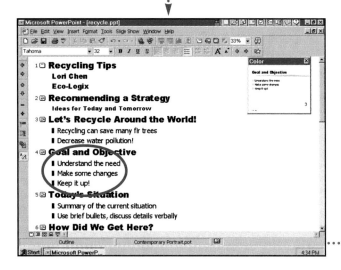

2 Select the first bulleted item under "What We Can Do" and type **Understand the need**. Select the second bulleted item and type **Make some changes**. Select the third bulleted item and type **Keep it up!**.

3 Click the **Slide View** button on the View toolbar to switch to Slide view. PowerPoint displays slide 3, the slide you changed.

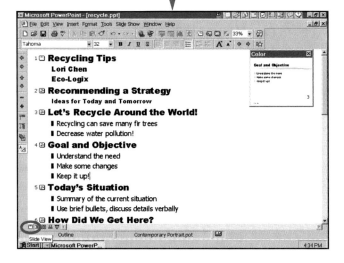

Puzzled?

If you see the wrong slide in Slide view, just click the **Next Slide** button (two down arrows) or the **Previous Slide** button (two up arrows) at the bottom of the vertical scroll bar to go to the correct slide.

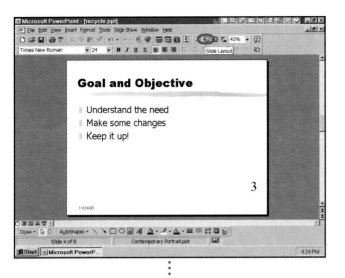

4 Click the **Slide Layout** button, and PowerPoint opens the Slide Layout dialog box.

Missing Link

You can click the scroll bars to see more AutoLayouts. You see 12 of PowerPoint's 24 AutoLayouts at one time. A black box outlines the AutoLayout that is selected, and the area below the buttons shows the title of the currently selected AutoLayout.

5 Select the AutoLayout you want to use. For example, click the **Text & Clip Art** AutoLayout in the lower-left corner. The AutoLayout's name appears in the lower-right corner of the dialog box. Click **Apply** to confirm your choice.

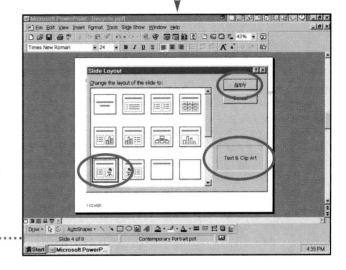

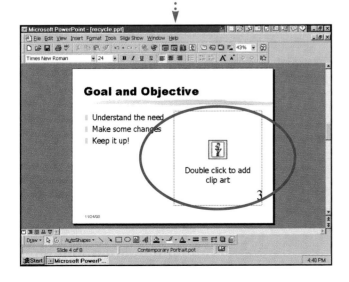

6 PowerPoint changes the current slide's layout, adding an AutoLayout that contains a placeholder for clip art. ■

TASK 60

Adding Clip Art

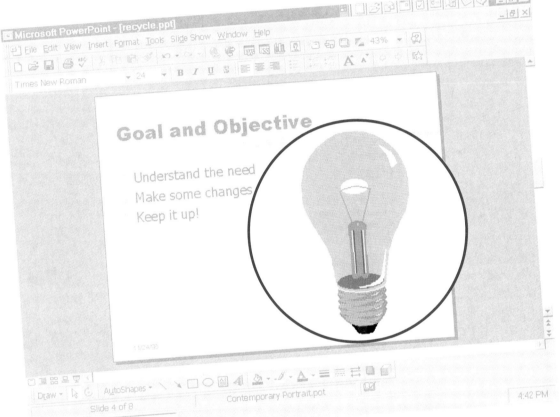

"Why would I do this?"

Clip art adds visual interest to your PowerPoint presentation. With PowerPoint's Clip Art Gallery, you can choose from more than 1,000 professionally prepared images. Adding a clip art image is easy when you're using one of PowerPoint's AutoLayouts.

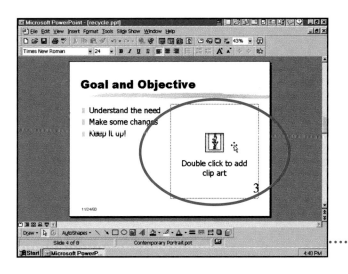

1 On slide 3, double-click the clip art placeholder (the icon that contains a picture of a man) on the right side of the slide. This selects the clip art placeholder. PowerPoint displays the Microsoft Clip Gallery dialog box.

2 Click the down scroll arrow in the Categories list box until you see the Clip Art category of your choice. Click **Industry** to select the energy clip art category.

Puzzled?

If you're using clip art for the first time, you may see a dialog box asking whether you would like to add the clip art images to PowerPoint. Click **OK**. This may take a few minutes.

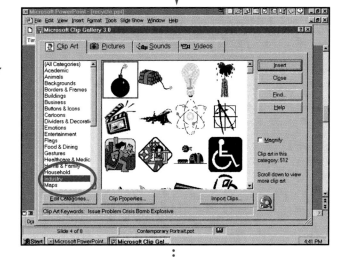

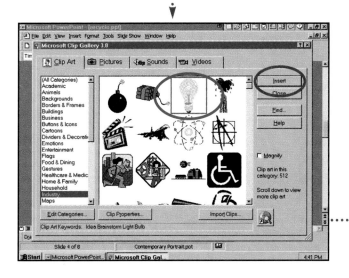

3 The box in the center shows each clip art image in the selected category. If necessary, use the scroll bar to find the image you want, and then click to select it. For this example, click the light bulb image.

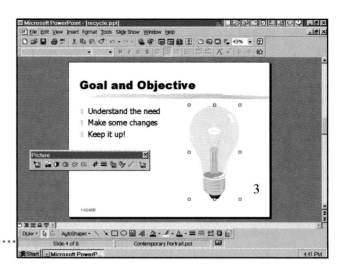

4 Click **Insert**, and PowerPoint adds the artwork to your presentation. The Picture toolbar also appears on-screen.

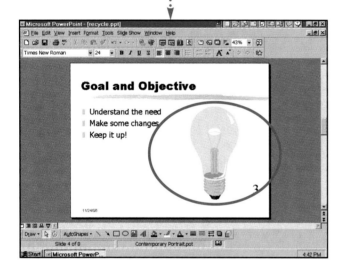

5 Press **Esc** to remove the resizing handles that surround the light bulb object and the Picture toolbar. ■

Creating a Table

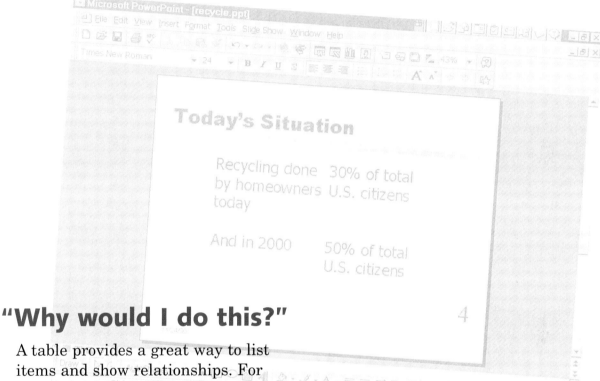

"Why would I do this?"

A table provides a great way to list items and show relationships. For presentations, use no more than two or three columns and three or four rows. If you need to show patterns in more complex data, use a graph. In PowerPoint, tables can contain figures, words, or both. After you create a table, you just click within a table box and type. PowerPoint automatically adjusts the size of the box to accommodate what you type.

Note that you must have Microsoft Word 97 installed in order to use the Table function.

1 Move to slide 4 (you can click the **Next Slide** button if you're working through these tasks in order) and click the bulleted list text area. PowerPoint displays the thick border and selection handles. Click the border and press **Deletc** twice to remove this text object and the bulleted list placeholder. Then click the **Insert Microsoft Word Table** button on the Standard toolbar. A table grid appears.

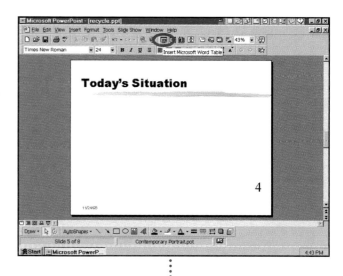

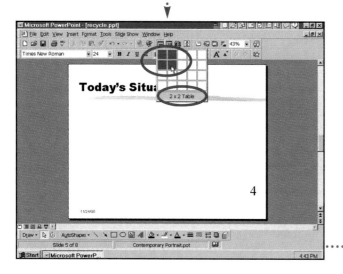

2 In the table grid, choose the number of rows and columns you want. With the mouse pointer on the box in the upper-left corner, press and hold the mouse button and drag to the right and downward to select two columns and two rows. You see 2 x 2 Table at the bottom of the table grid. This tells PowerPoint to create a two-column table with two rows.

3 When you release the mouse button, PowerPoint creates and opens the table in a special window. The table has four boxes, called *cells*, which are formed by the dotted lines.

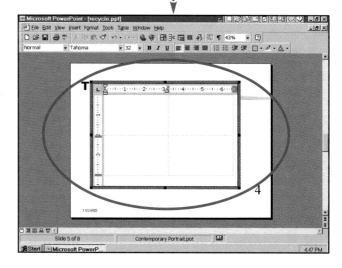

Puzzled?

If you create a table with the wrong number of columns or rows, click anywhere on the slide background to close the table, press **Delete** to remove the table, and repeat steps 1 and 2.

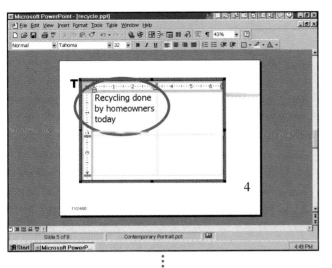

4 Click the upper-left cell and type **Recycling done by homeowners today**. Press **Enter** to insert a blank line below the text and enter the text in the upper-left cell.

5 Click the lower-left cell and type **And in 2000**. This enters text in the lower-left cell.

Puzzled?

If you need to edit the table to correct a mistake, double-click within the table area. You'll see the table window again, and you can make the changes you want. Then click the slide background to close the table.

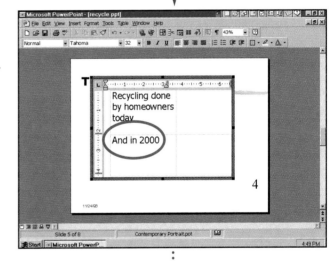

6 Click the upper-right cell and type **30% of total U.S. citizens**. Then click the lower-right cell and type **50% of total U.S. citizens**. This enters text in the top right and bottom right cells. Click the slide background to close the table window. Then press **Esc** to remove the resizing handles. ■

235

Creating a Chart

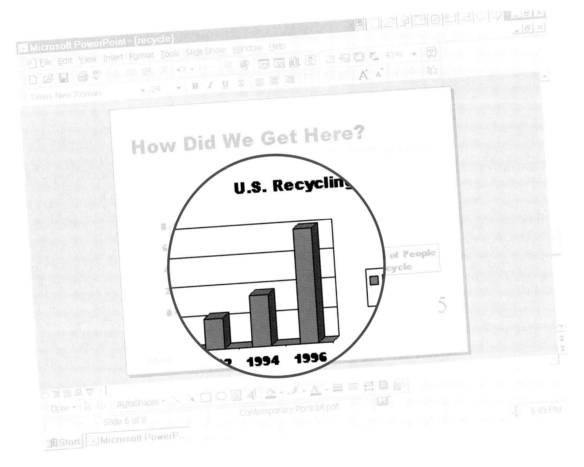

"Why would I do this?"

A table provides a handy way to summarize a few facts and figures. However, to show trends and comparisons in more complex data, it is better to use a chart.

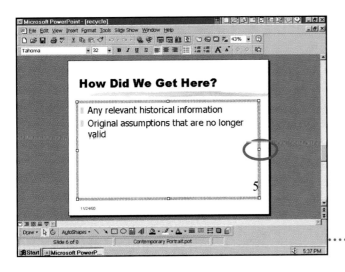

1 Select slide 5 (you can click the **Next Slide** button if you're working through these tasks in order). Click the bulleted list text area, and PowerPoint displays a thick border around it. Click the border to display the selection handles.

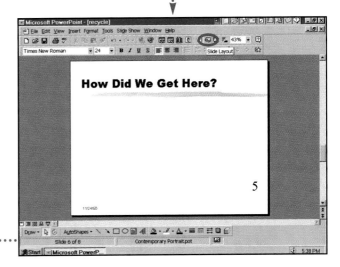

2 Press **Delete** twice to remove this text object and the bulleted list placeholder. Click the **Slide Layout** button, and you see the Slide Layout dialog box.

3 Click the Chart AutoLayout image in the second row, last column to select the Chart AutoLayout placeholder. Then click **Apply**. PowerPoint changes the slide to the Chart layout, and you see a chart placeholder.

4 Double-click the **Chart** icon in the center of the screen to activate the Chart icon. PowerPoint starts Microsoft Graph, and after a few moments, you see a datasheet. In the background, a chart appears on your slide.

> **Puzzled?**
>
> You don't have to use the data and the chart that Microsoft Graph has inserted. Graph provides them to give you something to work with. By making changes to this data, however, you can see how Graph works.

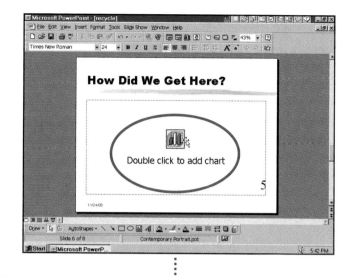

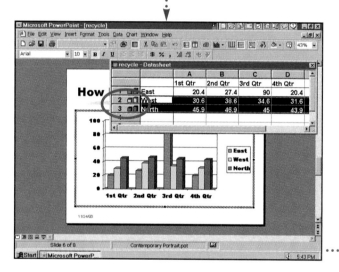

5 In the datasheet, click the **Row 2** button (the button with the 2 on it) and drag down to the **Row 3** button (to the left of row 3). This selects two rows of data that you don't need for your graph.

6 Press **Delete** to delete the data in rows 2 and 3. If necessary, click the datasheet's title bar and drag the datasheet window right and upward so that you can see the chart beneath.

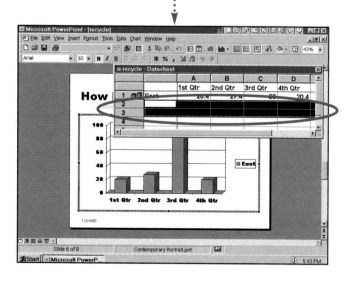

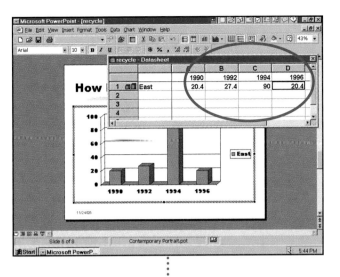

7 Click the cell just below A, type **1990**, and press **Tab** to move to the next cell to the right. Then type **1992** and press **Tab**, and type **1994** and press **Tab**. Finally, type **1996**. Press **Enter** to confirm the last entry. (See Task 36: "Entering Text and Numbers.") The text you type replaces the existing text, and Microsoft Graph adds the dates at the bottom of the graph.

8 Click the first cell in row 1 and type **Millions of People Who Recycle** (the row heading for row 1). Press **Tab** to move to cell A1. Then type **1.5** and press **Tab**; type **2.1** and press **Tab**; type **3.5** and press **Tab**; and type **7.8** (in Column D). Press **Enter** to confirm this last entry.

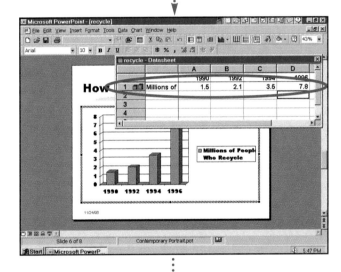

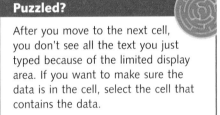

Puzzled?

After you move to the next cell, you don't see all the text you just typed because of the limited display area. If you want to make sure the data is in the cell, select the cell that contains the data.

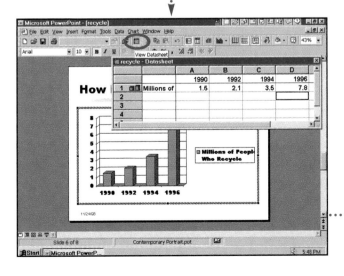

9 Click the **View Datasheet** button on the Graph toolbar to close the Datasheet window. Now you can see your chart. Notice the bars that represent data for each of the dates you have entered.

10 Open the **Chart** menu and choose **Chart Options**. You see the Chart Options dialog box.

Puzzled?

If you don't see a Chart Options command in the Chart menu, you probably clicked the slide background, which closed Microsoft Graph. To open Microsoft Graph again, double-click within the graph area.

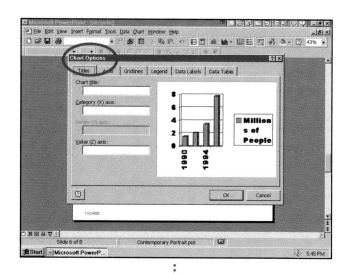

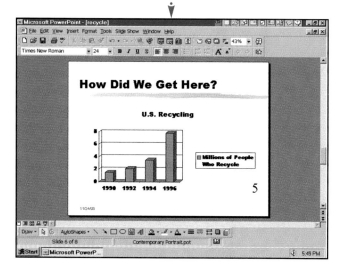

11 Click the **Chart Title** text box and type **U.S. Recycling**. Then click **OK**. This selects the Chart Title option. At the top of your graph, you see a title that echoes the text you typed at the beginning of row 1—Millions of People Who Recycle.

12 Click the slide background. This completes your graph and returns you to PowerPoint. Press **Esc** to remove the resizing handles. ■

Adding Speaker's Notes

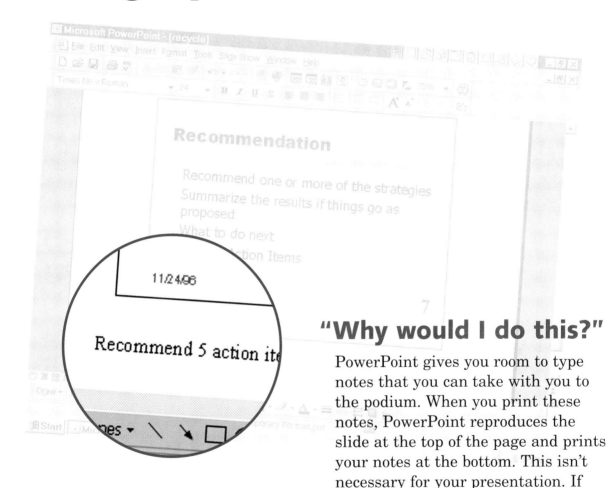

"Why would I do this?"

PowerPoint gives you room to type notes that you can take with you to the podium. When you print these notes, PowerPoint reproduces the slide at the top of the page and prints your notes at the bottom. This isn't necessary for your presentation. If you prefer, you can place your notes on 3 x 5 cards or paper; however, consider using PowerPoint to make your notes right after you create each slide. Then the decisions you made when you created the slide are still fresh in your mind.

1 In Slide view, select the slide to which you want to add notes. For example, display slide 7: Recommendation. Then click the **Notes Pages View** button on the View toolbar. You see what your note pages will look like when PowerPoint prints them: the slide is reproduced on the top of the screen, with space for your notes on the bottom.

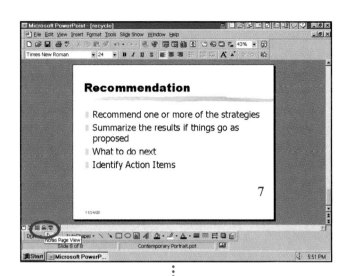

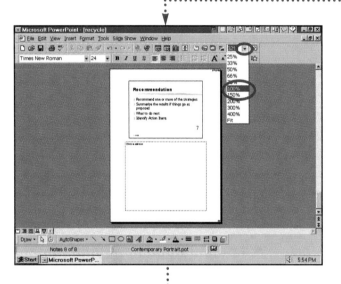

2 Click the **Zoom** drop-down arrow on the Standard toolbar, and choose **100%** in the zoom percentages list. This magnifies the screen so that you can see what you're writing.

> **Puzzled?**
>
> Need to make a change to your notes? No problem! Just redisplay the slide to which you have added the notes, and then choose the **View, Notes Pages** command.

3 Click within the notes area and type the note that appears in this figure. Click the **Slide View** button on the View toolbar, and PowerPoint hides your notes. ■

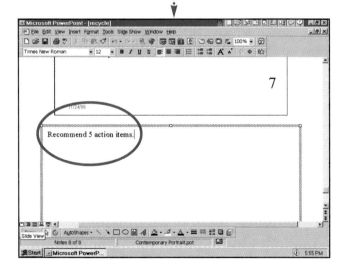

Setting Up the Slides

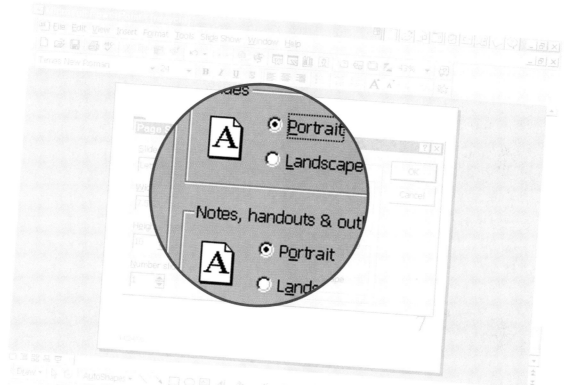

"Why would I do this?"

Before you print your slides, set up your slides by telling PowerPoint what type of output you intend to produce. You can choose from on-screen slide show (electronic presentation), letter-sized paper, A4 (European) paper, 35mm slides, and custom sizes. If you want to print overhead transparencies, you should choose one of the paper sizes (letter or A4).

1 Open the **File** menu and choose **Page Setup**. PowerPoint displays the Page Sctup dialog box.

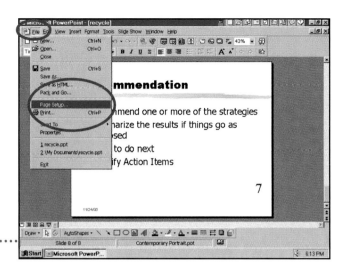

2 In the **Slides Sized For** drop-down list box, click **Letter Paper (8.5x11 in)**. This selects the letter-size paper option.

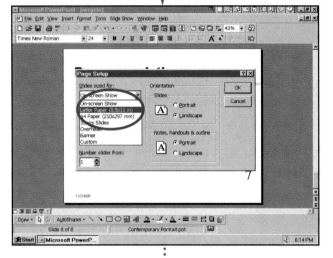

Puzzled?

Looking for the Overhead transparencies option? Choose one of the paper options (**letter** or **A4**). For an electronic presentation, choose **On-screen Show**. If you want to produce 35mm slides, choose **35mm Slides**. You can send your PowerPoint slide files to a service bureau (i.e., Genigraphics) for overnight printing of 35mm slides, digital color overheads, large display prints, and posters.

3 Click **Portrait** in the Slides area to print overheads without clipping off the sides of your transparencies. Click **OK**. PowerPoint adjusts your slides to reflect the changes you have made. ■

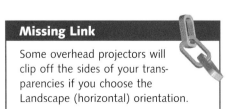

Missing Link

Some overhead projectors will clip off the sides of your transparencies if you choose the Landscape (horizontal) orientation.

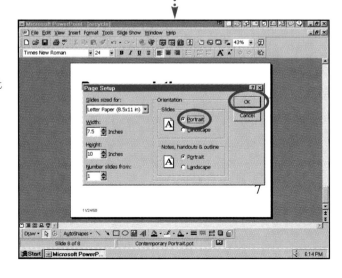

Running a Slide Show

"Why would I do this?"

Perhaps the best way to give a
PowerPoint presentation is to create
an electronic presentation on-screen.
Your slides appear in vivid color. You
can use the mouse pointer to point
out features of your slides. You can
even draw and write on the screen.

1 With the RECYCLE.PPT presentation on-screen, click the **Slide Sorter View** button on the View toolbar. This switches to Slide Sorter view. Then click the first slide to select it.

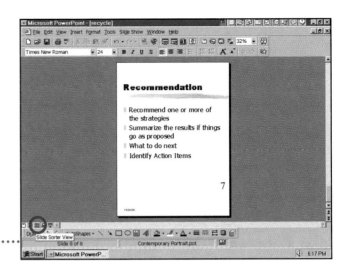

2 Click the **Slide Show** button on the View toolbar. PowerPoint zooms the slide so that it takes over the screen.

3 Click the left mouse button or press **Spacebar** to advance to the next slide. Then click the right mouse button or press **Backspace** to return to the previous slide.

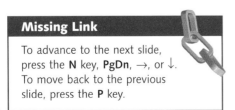

Missing Link

To advance to the next slide, press the **N** key, **PgDn**, →, or ↓. To move back to the previous slide, press the **P** key.

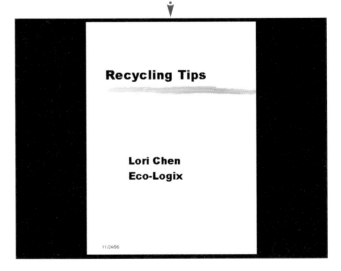

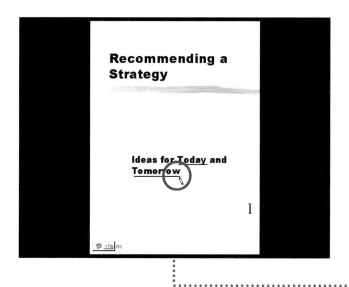

4 Click the right mouse button to display the shortcut menu. Click **Pen**, and the mouse pointer changes to a pen shape. Press and hold the mouse button and drag the mouse pointer pen to write or draw on the slide with the mouse.

Missing Link

To return to the arrow mouse pointer, click to display the shortcut menu and choose **Arrow**.

5 Continue until you have viewed all the slides. Then press **Esc** to stop viewing slides before you reach the last slide. You see Slide Sorter view again. ■

Puzzled?

The writing or drawing you make this way is temporary; it does not affect the slide's appearance after the slide show is over.

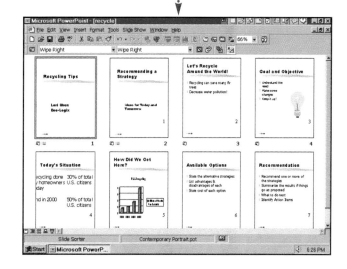

PART
X

Using Microsoft Outlook

MICROSOFT OUTLOOK IS MICROSOFT EXCHANGE (the Windows message system) and Microsoft Schedule+, plus more—and all rolled into one personal information manager program. Outlook functions like a 3-ring binder that you might tote around during your business day.

Outlook can help you keep track of e-mail, daily appointments, and meetings, prioritize your work, and much more. Whether you are working on an individual computer or computers linked together in workgroups, you can use Outlook to manage your time.

Here's what you'll find in Outlook:

- *Inbox:* You can send and receive e-mail and faxes, preview messages before you open them, and mark messages with message flags to follow up on any action necessary.

- *Calendar:* You can schedule and keep track of appointments, events, holidays, and meetings or even set up meetings. Also, you can set up a reminder—an alarm that beeps to remind you of an appointment. The Date Navigator helps you find and view information in your schedule.

- *Contact List:* You can build a contact list that contains names, addresses, phone numbers, and e-mail addresses. You can sort and store the contacts in various ways. For instance, you can store several addresses, phone numbers, and e-mail addresses for each contact. You can also go to a contact's Web page on the World Wide Web.

- *To Do List:* You can organize your daily or weekly projects and tasks in one place, as well as prioritize tasks and assign tasks. The TaskPad lets you see the day's tasks and schedule time to work on them.

- *Journal:* Record interactions with important contacts, record Outlook items such as e-mail messages, or files that arc important to you, an appointment, task, or note.

- *Notes:* Notes are the electronic version of paper sticky notes. You can use notes to jot down ideas, reminders, questions, instructions, and anything you might write as a note on paper. You can leave notes open on-screen as you work.

- *Files:* If you're working on a computer that is linked to a workgroup, you can access, view, and share files from within Outlook.

This part shows you how to use Outlook to computerize your daily appointments, contacts, tasks, projects, journal entries, and sticky notes.

TASK

66

Managing the Inbox

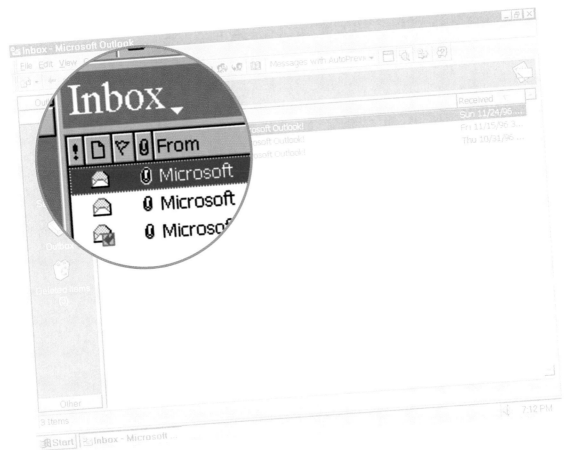

"Why would I do this?"

Outlook's Inbox enables you to send and receive electronic messages and faxes from the office, home, or when you're on the road. You can even preview messages in the Inbox window before you open them. The Inbox also lets you use flags to mark messages for further action.

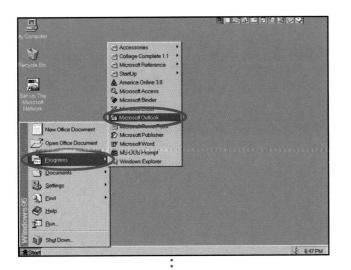

1 Start Outlook. If you see the Choose Profile dialog box, open the **Profile Name** drop-down list and make a selection. Then click **OK**.

Puzzled?

If no Profile name exists, you will have to create one. In the Windows Control Panel, double-click the **Mail** icon, click the **Services** tab, and click **Show Profiles**. Then click the **General** tab and click **Add**, and the Inbox Setup Wizard will walk you through creating a Profile name.

2 Click **OK** to remove the Office Assistant from your screen.

Missing Link

By default, the Messages with AutoPreview option is turned on so that you can see the first few lines of messages you haven't read. To turn off this option, select the **View**, **Current View** command and choose a different view.

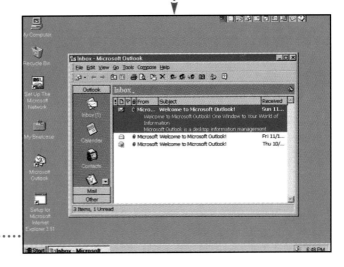

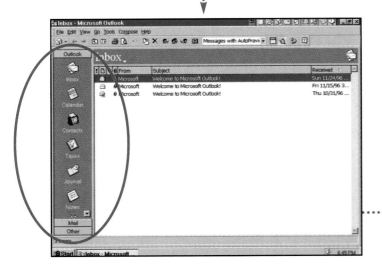

3 Click the **Maximize** button in the upper-right corner of the Outlook window to make it a full screen. The Outlook toolbar appears on the left side of the window. The Inbox icon at the top of the toolbar shows you the number of unread messages. You can see the first few lines of text in any message you haven't read.

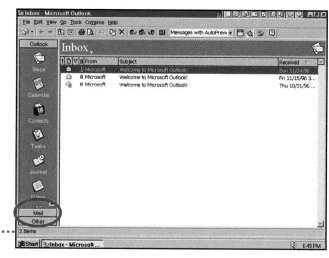

4 Click the **Mail** button at the bottom of the Outlook toolbar to display the Mail toolbar. The icons on the Mail toolbar show the number of unread messages, messages sent, and messages in the outbox (outgoing mail), and deleted items in the Outlook recycle bin.

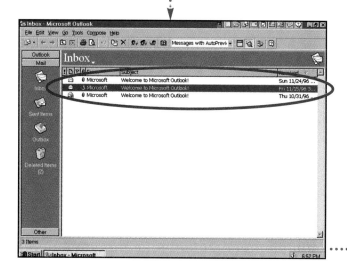

5 Double-click a message to open it. You see the Message dialog box.

6 Click the down arrow at the bottom of the vertical scroll bar to view the entire message. When you finish reading the message, click the **Reply** button on the Message toolbar.

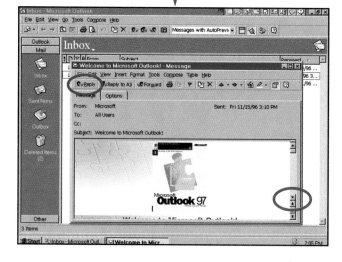

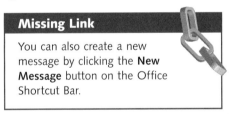

7 The recipient's name appears in the To text box, and the subject appears in the Subject text box. Enter a carbon copy name in the **CC** text box, if desired. The original message appears in the lower portion of the message area. Click in the top of the message area and type a response to the message. When you're finished, click the **Send** button on the Message toolbar to send the message to the Outbox.

8 To compose a new message, open the **Compose** menu and choose **New Mail Message**. The Untitled - Message window appears. Fill in the To, CC, and Subject text boxes and enter your message in the message area. Then click the **Send** button on the Message toolbar to send the message to the Outbox.

> **Missing Link**
>
> You can also create a new message by clicking the **New Message** button on the Office Shortcut Bar.

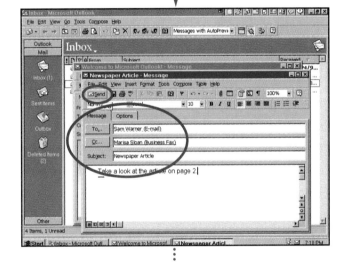

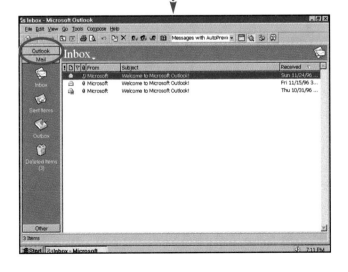

9 Click the **Close** (X) button on each message window to close all the message windows. When you finish, click the Outbox button on the Outlook toolbar to look at your outgoing mail. Then click the **Outlook** button at the top of the Mail toolbar to return to the Outlook toolbar.

Scheduling Appointments and Events

"Why would I do this?"

You can fill in daily and weekly appointments and events in your schedule. For example, you might want to track interviews, meetings, doctor and dentist appointments, and events (such as birthdays, anniversaries, and conferences). The time schedule displays a 24-hour day from 12:00 a.m. to 11:00 p.m. You can assign a reminder to an appointment so that you don't miss the appointment.

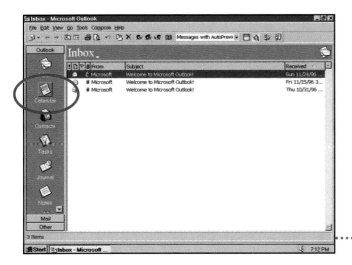

1 Click the **Calendar** button on the Outlook toolbar. You see the Calendar daily schedule, which is the Day/Week/Month view.

Puzzled?

If you're in the wrong view, click the **Current View** drop-down arrow on the Calendar toolbar and choose the view you want.

2 The large numbers on the left side of the daily schedule represent the hours of the day. Next to that, you see 30-minute time slots. The current month and next month calendars appear in the upper-right corner of the window. Click the **12 pm** time slot.

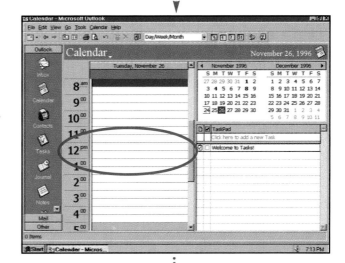

Missing Link

To set a new appointment, click the **New Appointment** button on the Office Shortcut Bar.

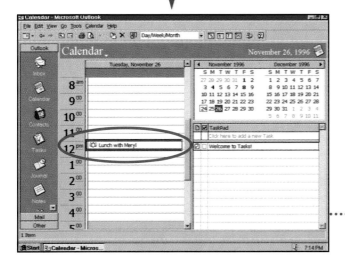

3 In the 12 pm time slot, type **Lunch with Meryl**. Then press **Enter**. The appointment text appears, with a Reminder icon (a tiny bell) next to it.

Missing Link

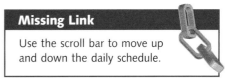

Use the scroll bar to move up and down the daily schedule.

257

4 Click the **1:00** (p.m.) time slot and drag down to the **2:00** (p.m.) time slot. Release the mouse button. This selects three time slots. Type **Staff Meeting** and press **Enter**. You see the appointment is set for one-and-a-half hours.

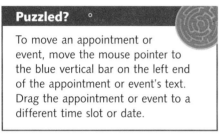

Puzzled?

To move an appointment or event, move the mouse pointer to the blue vertical bar on the left end of the appointment or event's text. Drag the appointment or event to a different time slot or date.

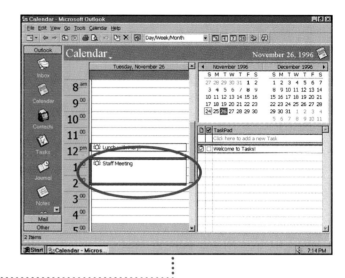

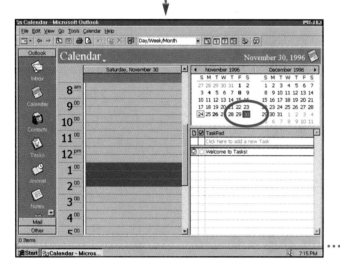

5 Click the Saturday date in the current week on the current month calendar. This selects a different day.

6 Double-click the **8:00** (a.m.) time slot, and the Appointment dialog box opens.

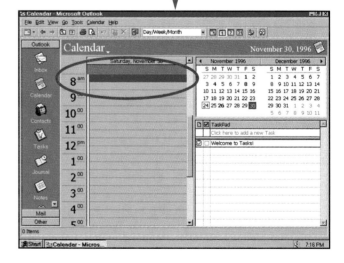

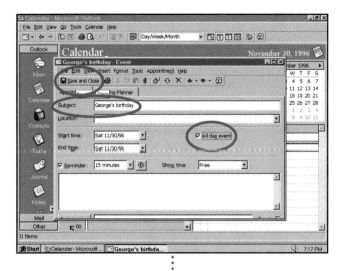

7 Type **George's birthday** in the **Subject** text box. This enters the event subject. Then click the **All Day Event** check box to change the appointment to an event. By default, a reminder is set for every appointment and event; an alarm bell will sound every fifteen minutes. Click the **Save and Close** button.

Missing Link

To remove a reminder, double-click an appointment or event and click the **Reminder** check box.

8 Outlook saves the event, adds it to the schedule, and closes the Event dialog box. The Reminder icon, (a tiny bell) appears next to the birthday event on Friday at 8:00 a.m. ▦

Missing Link

Outlook displays a reminder dialog box, and you hear a bell ring to remind you about an appointment or event. You can click **Dismiss** to remove the reminder; click **Postpone** to delay the reminder; or change the Reminder time interval.

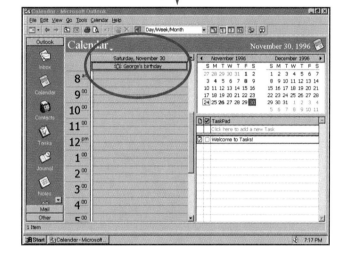

Viewing Your Schedule

"Why would I do this?"

The Date Navigator feature lets you switch the view from today's schedule to a different day, a week at-a-glance, or a month schedule. You can schedule appointments and events in any view, and you can move the appointments and events.

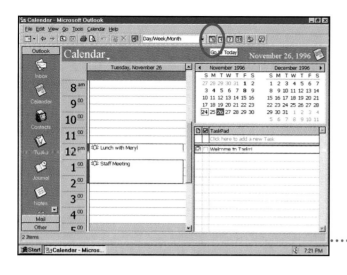

1 Click the **Go To Today** button on the Calendar toolbar to see today's daily schedule.

2 The appointments and events you have scheduled for today appear.

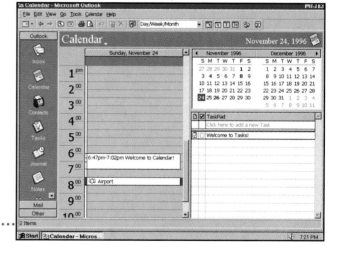

3 Click the **Week** button on the Calendar toolbar to see the weekly schedule.

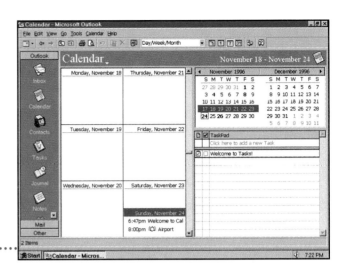

4 In the weekly schedule, the days of the week show as Monday through Sunday. Outlook displays the appointments in normal text and displays the event in a gray box.

5 Click the **Month** button on the Calendar toolbar.

6 The monthly schedule appears, starting with the last day of the previous month and ending with the first day of the next month. Today's date contains a blue bar, and the weekend days are listed in a column on the right. ■

Puzzled?

If your appointment is too long to read in the Week or Month view, click the **Day** button or the **Go To Today** button on the Calendar toolbar to read it all.

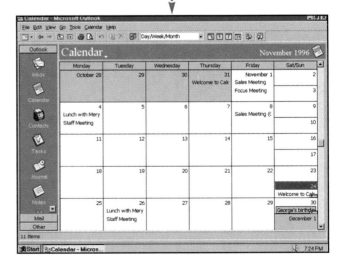

Planning a Meeting

"Why would I do this?"

The Meeting Planner enables you to plan a meeting from start to finish. You specify the attendees, determine a meeting time, check for any schedule conflicts, and then schedule a room. You also can send a memo to each attendee inviting them to the meeting.

Task 69: Planning a Meeting

1 Click the **Plan a Meeting** button on the Calendar toolbar. The Plan a Meeting dialog box appears.

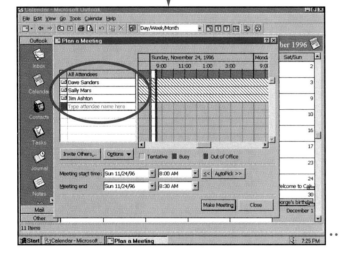

2 Enter the attendees' names in the All Attendees list. Type **Dave Sanders** where you see Type attendee name here. Then press **Enter**, type **Sally Mars**, press **Enter**, type **Jim Ashton**, and press **Enter**.

Missing Link

All the people you invite to the meeting must be using Microsoft Outlook to know about the meeting.

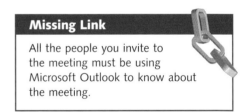

3 Choose a date, such as Friday, from the **Meeting Start Time** date drop-down list. Then choose a meeting start time and end time—8 a.m. and 9 a.m. Click the **Make Meeting** button. The Meeting dialog box appears.

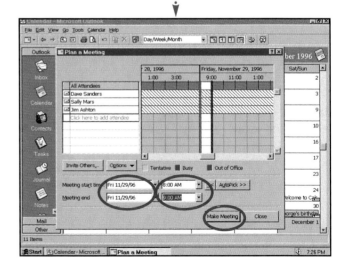

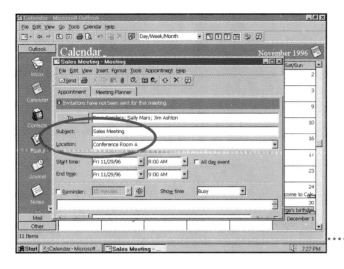

4 Type **Sales Meeting** in the Subject text box, press **Tab**, and type **Conference Room A** in the Location text box.

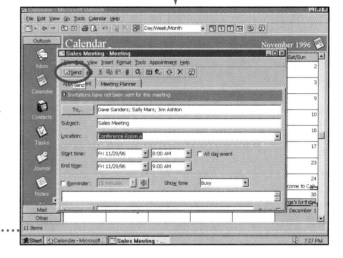

5 Click the **Send** button on the Meeting toolbar. This sends a memo regarding the meeting to all attendees who are invited.

6 In the Calendar, click the **Friday** date on the current month calendar, and then click the **Day** button on the Calendar toolbar. The Sales Meeting is scheduled at 8:00 a.m., as indicated by a Meeting icon (with two people's heads). ■

Creating a To Do List

"Why would I do this?"

The To Do List helps you organize tasks and projects that are significant to the various dates and appointments on your schedule. You can build lists of daily things you need to do and items you must work on to complete a project. Any item you list in the To Do List is called a task.

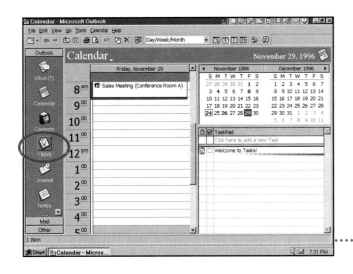

1 Click the **Tasks** button on the Calendar toolbar. This selects the Go Tasks command. The Tasks view appears.

2 Click in the column below Click here to add a new task. Type **Review contract** and press **Enter**. Then type **Review profit and loss statement**, press **Enter**, type **Review tax forms**, and press **Enter**. This enters descriptions of the tasks. (Outlook displays the tasks in reverse order.)

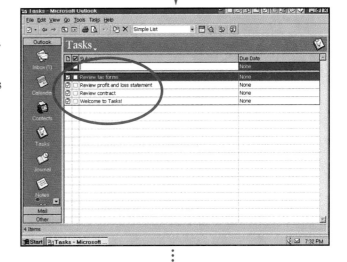

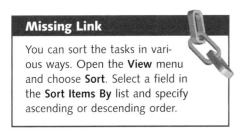

Missing Link

You can sort the tasks in various ways. Open the **View** menu and choose **Sort**. Select a field in the **Sort Items By** list and specify ascending or descending order.

3 Click in the Due Date column next to the first task. Then click the drop-down arrow to display the current month calendar and click a date in the calendar. Repeat this step for the other tasks. This specifies the due date for each task.

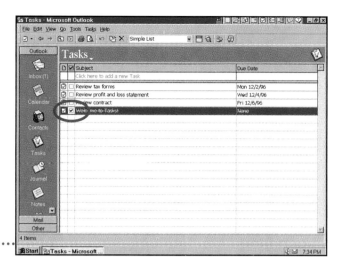

4 Click the empty check box next to a task description. A line is drawn through the task, indicating that thc task is complete.

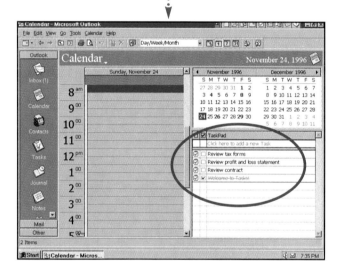

5 Click the **Calendar** button on the Outlook toolbar to return to the Calendar view. As you can see here, the tasks are listed on the right side of the schedule. ▪

Tracking Tasks

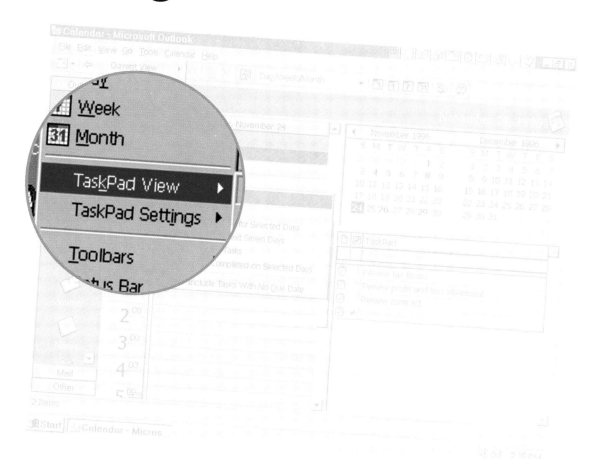

"Why would I do this?"

After you add tasks to your To Do List, you may want to track the tasks. You can view the tasks in various ways with TaskPad: you can view all tasks, today's tasks, active tasks for selected days, tasks for the next seven days, overdue tasks, and tasks completed on selected days.

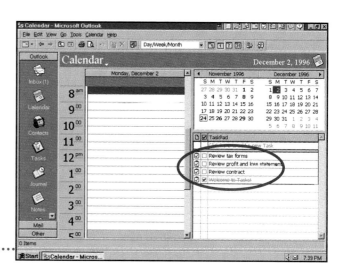

1 In Calendar view, open the **View** menu, choose **TaskPad View**, and click **Today's Tasks**. Notice the tasks that start today in the To Do List on the right side of the schedule.

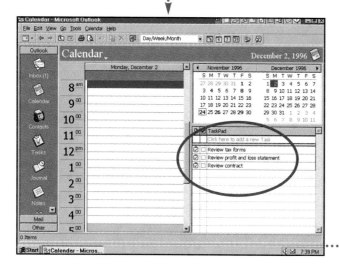

2 Click the first task's due date on the current month calendar. Then open the **View** menu, choose **TaskPad View**, and click **Active Tasks for Selected Days**. Outlook displays only the tasks that are active for the selected day.

3 Open the **View** menu, choose **TaskPad View**, and click **All Tasks**. Notice all the tasks are listed in the To Do List. ■

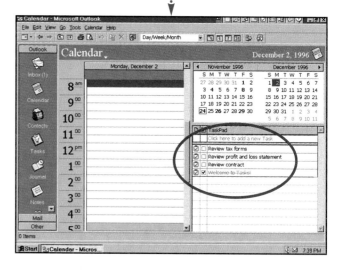

Creating a Contacts List

"Why would I do this?"

You can build a contact list that contains business and personal contact information. The list is an electronic version of an address book or Rolodex card file. Once you set up the names, addresses, phone numbers, and e-mail addresses, you can use the contacts to create mailing lists and dial up other computers with a modem.

Task 72: Creating a Contacts List

1 In Calendar view, click the **Contacts** button on the Outlook toolbar. This selects the Go Contacts command. You see the Contacts view—a blank address book with tabs dividing it into alphabetical sections.

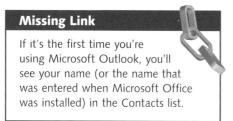

Missing Link

If it's the first time you're using Microsoft Outlook, you'll see your name (or the name that was entered when Microsoft Office was installed) in the Contacts list.

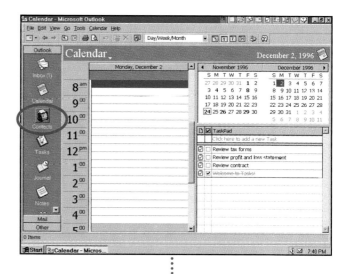

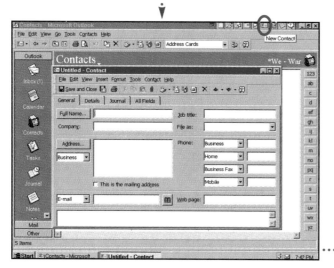

2 Click the **New Contact** button on the Office Shortcut bar. The Contact dialog box appears.

3 Type the contact information that appears in the figure for step 4. Fill in the text boxes, pressing **Tab** to move between boxes. When you finish, click the **Save and New** button on the Contacts toolbar. Repeat this step twice to add two more contacts to the Contacts list. Then click the **Close** (X) button to close the Contact dialog box.

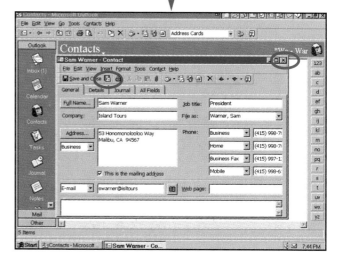

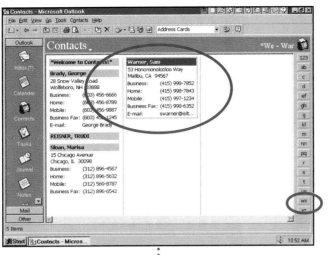

4 Click the **WX** tab on the right side of the Contacts list. Outlook finds and highlights the first contact whose name begins with the letter W.

Puzzled?

To delete a contact, click the contact to select it, and then click the **Delete** button on the Contacts toolbar.

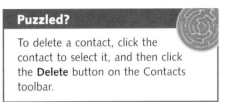

5 Click the **Current View** drop-down arrow and click **Phone List**. This selects the Phone List view. You see the contact information in a grid.

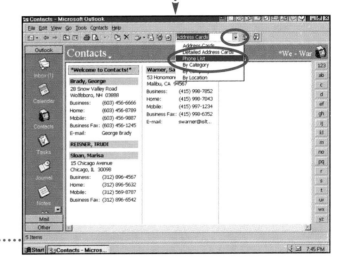

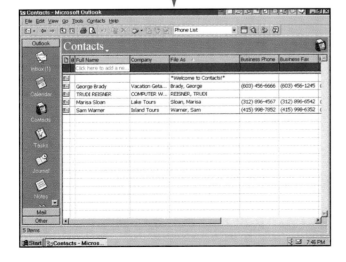

6 Use the scroll bars to view all the contact information in the grid.

273

Creating a Journal

"Why would I do this?"

The Journal feature lets you record information that is important to you so you can keep it together in one place. You might record an activity (such as an interaction with a contact), a mail message, file, appointment, task, or note.

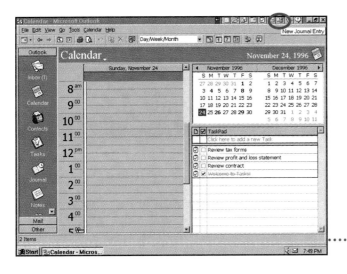

1 In Calendar view, click the **New Journal Entry** button in the Office Shortcut bar. The Journal dialog box appears.

2 Type **Sales Call** in the Subject text box. Then choose the Entry Type, such as **Phone Call**. Type **Sam Warner** in the Contact text box, press **Tab**, and type **Island Tours** in the Company text box.

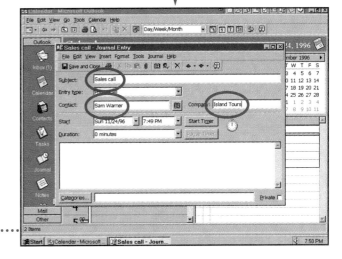

3 Click the **Start Timer** button. Outlook starts the timer and begins to track the duration of your journal entry.

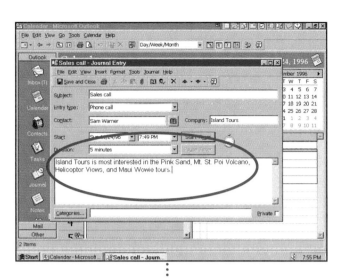

4 In the box at the bottom of the Journal Entry dialog box, type **Island Tours is most interested in the Pink Sand, Mt. St. Poi Volcano, Helicopter Views, and Maui Wowie tours**. This manually records an item in your journal. Click the **Pause Timer** button to stop the timer. The elapsed time is displayed in the Duration box.

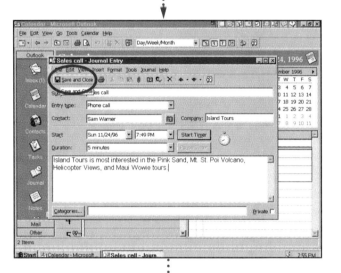

5 Click the **Save and Close** button on the Journal toolbar, and Outlook saves the journal entry and closes the dialog box.

> **Puzzled?**
>
> To delete a journal entry, in Journal view, right-click the journal entry you want to delete and click **Delete** on the shortcut menu.

6 Click the **Journal** button on the Outlook toolbar to open the Journal view. There you see a list of the journal entries. ■

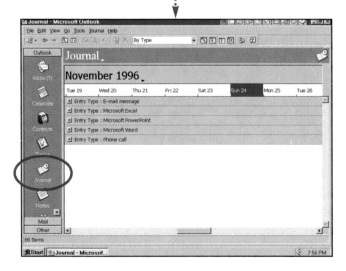

Creating Notes

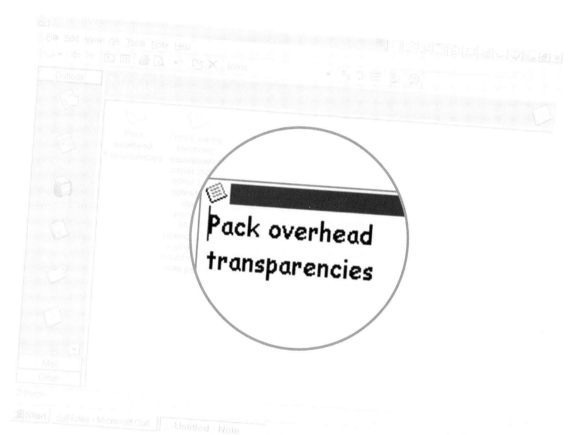

"Why would I do this?"

With notes, you can jot down ideas, questions, reminders, directions, and any note you would write on note paper. You can leave notes visible on-screen as you work.

Task 74: Creating Notes

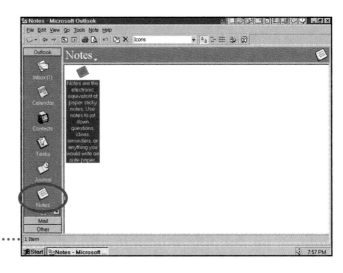

1 In Calendar view, click the **Notes** button on the Outlook Toolbar. You see the Notes view.

2 Click the **New Note** button on the Office Shortcut bar, and the Note box appears.

> ### Missing Link
>
> To open a note, double-click the note in Note view. To resize an open note, drag the lower-right corner of the note.

3 Type **Pack overhead transparencies** in the Note box. Leave the note open on-screen for now. (When you are ready to close the note, click the **Close** (X) button on the Note.) ■

> ### Puzzled?
>
> To delete an open note, click the **Note** icon in the upper-left corner of the note and choose **Delete** from the shortcut menu.

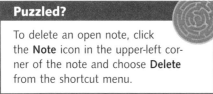

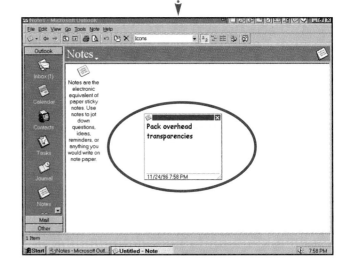

PART
XI

Using Microsoft Office and the World Wide Web

▲ ● ■ ▲ ● ■ ▲ ●

YOU CAN PUBLISH A MICROSOFT Office document as a Web page so that other people on the World Wide Web can see your document. In order to place Web pages on the Web, you need to have an Internet Service Provider that provides you with space for Web pages or access to a Web server established at your company. You can find out from the Webmaster (or the person who manages the Web servers) where to place your Web pages.

This part shows you how to publish a Word document as a Web page. When you save a Word document as a Web page, Word closes the document and then reopens it in HTML (HyperText Markup Language) format.

Every Web page is basically a plain text file with formatting instructions for the text, graphics, and links added to it. This file is called the HTML source because the instructions are written in HTML format. The Web recognizes the HTML format and displays the Web page similarly to how you would see it in Word's Online Layout View.

The Online Layout View in Word lets you see your document as it will look in a Web browser. This view makes the text easy to read because it's large and wraps to fit the window.

After you convert a Word document to a Web page, you can publish your Web page on the Internet by sending the page to an FTP (File Transfer Protocol) site on the Internet. FTP is a protocol that the Internet uses to send files between your computer and other computers on the Internet. Computers that offer files for download are called FTP sites. Using FTP is a fast and reliable way to download files from other Internet computers and to upload files for yourself. In this part, you learn how to send a Web page to an FTP site.

Suppose you have an order form that was created in Excel. The Internet could provide some customers to purchase products from your company. You could convert the order form into HTML format and publish it on the Web so that Internet users could complete the form to make purchases. HTML format includes instructions that are written using the Hypertext Markup Language and recognized by the Web.

To convert an Excel worksheet and chart into HTML format and publish it on the Web, use the File Save As HTML command. Then the Internet Assistant Wizard takes over and guides you through the steps of converting the data to a Web page. The wizard enables you to create a new Web page or add data to an existing one. You can specify the ranges in the worksheet and the charts that you want to include and exclude on a Web page. You also design the layout of your Web page and specify the name and location of the Web page on the Internet.

In PowerPoint, you can convert a slide show into HTML format and publish it on the Web. Just like in Excel, you can use the File Save As HTML command. Then the Internet Assistant takes over and guides you through the steps of converting the slide show to a Web page.

If the Save As HTML command appears dimmed in Excel's or PowerPoint's File menu, you must install the add-in program called the Internet Assistant. Once you do, the Internet Assistant will walk you through the process of saving in HTML format.

You can browse the Web while you're in any Office program. The Web toolbar provides tools for browsing Web pages backward and forward, refreshing the current page, searching the Web, storing Web pages in the Favorite Places folder, and entering a URL.

When you're working in Microsoft Outlook's Contacts list, you can view a contact's Web page. The contact's information must include a Web page URL (Uniform Resource Locator). A URL is similar to a file name that the Web will use to search and locate the Web page.

TASK

75

Publishing a Word Document As a Web Page

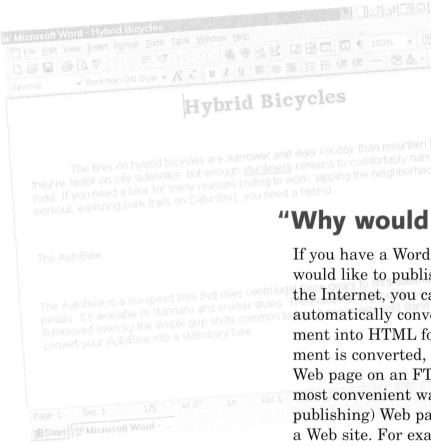

"Why would I do this?"

If you have a Word document that you would like to publish as a Web page on the Internet, you can do just that. Word automatically converts your Word document into HTML format. Once the document is converted, you can place the Web page on an FTP site, which is the most convenient way of uploading (or publishing) Web pages you've created to a Web site. For example, you might want to publish a company newsletter or product brochure on the Internet. After you publish the document, you see the document as it would appear in a Web browser. Then you can get on the Internet and view your Web page. Other users will be able to view your Web page, too.

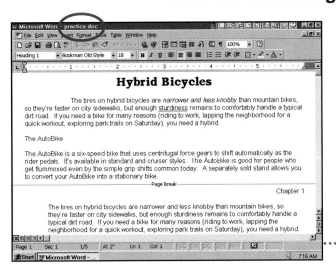

1 Start Word (as described in Task 1: "Starting and Exiting Microsoft Office 97 Programs"). Open the document you want to convert, such as the PRACTICE.DOC document.

2 Open the **File** menu and choose **Save As HTML**. The Save As HTML dialog box opens, and the HTML Document choice appears in the Save As Type list.

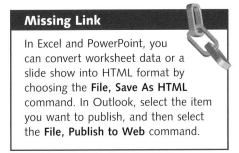

Missing Link

In Excel and PowerPoint, you can convert worksheet data or a slide show into HTML format by choosing the **File, Save As HTML** command. In Outlook, select the item you want to publish, and then select the **File, Publish to Web** command.

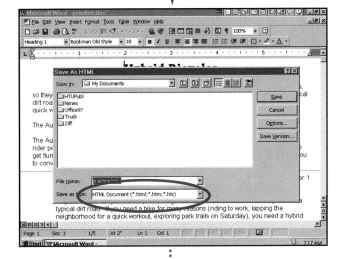

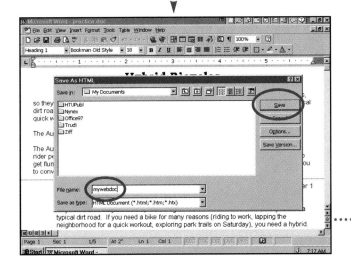

3 In the Save In list, choose a location for your document, if desired. Then type **mywebdoc** in the File Name text box. Click **Save**. This converts the document to HTML format so it can be published on the Web.

4 The document appears with the name HYBRID BICYCLES in the title bar. This name is the title of the document.

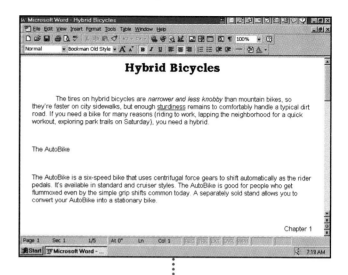

Puzzled?

HTML automatically adds blank lines under paragraphs and headings. If you have too much white space in your Web page, you can prevent ending up with too many blank lines in your Web page. Open the **Format** menu, choose **Paragraph**, and increase the number of points in the **After** box in the Spacing area.

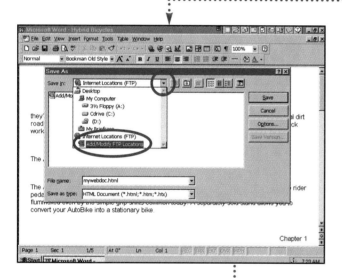

5 To tell Word about the FTP sites you want to access, open the **File** menu and choose **Save As**. In the Save As dialog box, click the **Save In** drop-down arrow and click **Add/Modify FTP Locations**.

6 In the **Name of FTP Site** text box, type **ftp://** and the FTP site name. Or, click an address in the FTP sites box. For example, use **FTP://ftp.mcp.com** (Macmillan Computer Publishing). This tells Word the name of the computer at the FTP site.

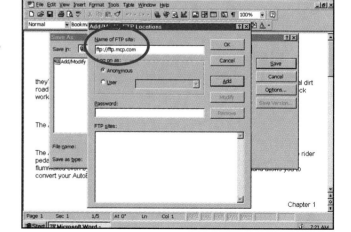

Missing Link

FTP addresses begin with FTP://. If you don't know the correct FTP site name, ask the site's system administrator.

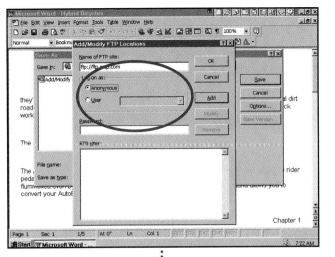

7 If you have a personal account at the FTP site, click the **User** option button in the Log On As area. Then enter your user name and password. If you don't have a personal account, click **Anonymous**.

Puzzled?

Anonymous users are given access to only certain public areas of a site. In most cases, you connect as an anonymous user if you want to download files; an anonymous user may not be able to upload files.

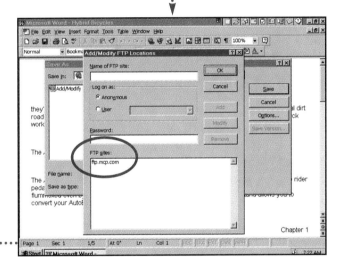

8 Click the **Add** button to add the FTP site. As you can see, the new FTP site appears in the FTP Sites box at the bottom of the Add/Modify FTP Locations dialog box.

9 Click **OK**, and the name of the new FTP site appears in the Save In box.

10 To send a Web page from Word to an FTP site, connect to the Internet. In Word, in the Save As dialog box, click the FTP location you want. You might try **ftp://ftp.mcp.com** for example.

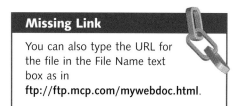

Missing Link

You can also type the URL for the file in the File Name text box as in ftp://ftp.mcp.com/mywebdoc.html.

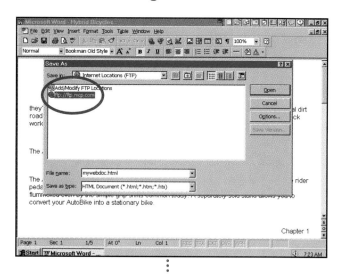

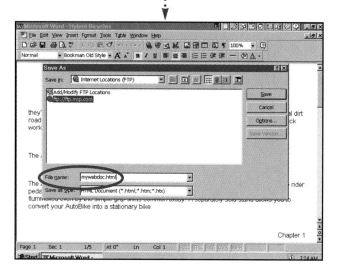

11 Type the HTML file name in the **File Name** text box. For this example, type **MYWEBDOC.HTML**. Click **Save**, and Word uploads the file to the FTP site. ■

Viewing a Document in Word's Online Layout View

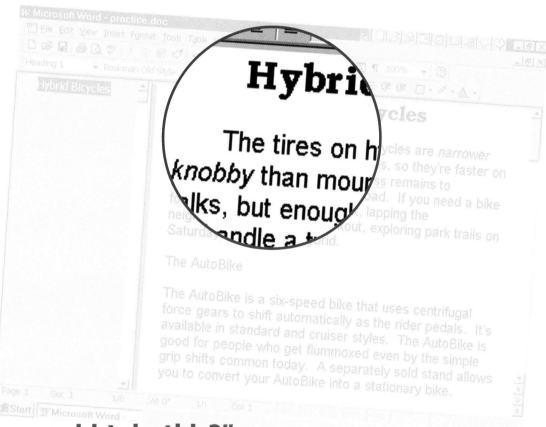

"Why would I do this?"

You can view any document in Word's Online Layout View. This view shows a version of the Web page that is similar to what it will look like in a Web browser. Your Web page might look different in a browser such as Netscape, Internet Explorer, or America Online than it does in Word, depending on how your browser interprets HTML codes. The text is large and wraps to the View window so that you can see the end of every line of text (not the way it wraps for printing where you might not see some text on the far right).

Task 76: Viewing a Document in Word's Online Layout View

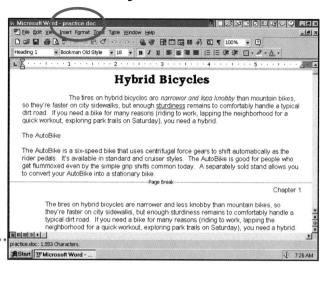

1 In Word, open the PRACTICE.DOC file.

2 Click the **Online Layout View** button on the left end of the status bar to switch to that view.

3 As you can see here, the document contains large text and wraps to the window so that you can see the end of every line of text. Use the scroll bars to see the rest of the document.

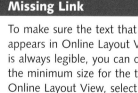

Missing Link

To make sure the text that appears in Online Layout View is always legible, you can change the minimum size for the text. In Online Layout View, select the **Tools, Options** command and click the **View** tab. Enter the minimum font size you want in the **Enlarge Fonts Less Than** box. The default font size is 12 points.

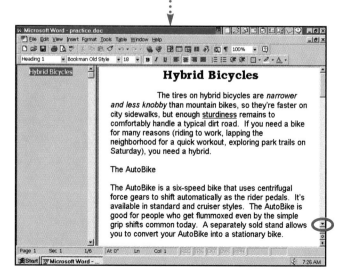

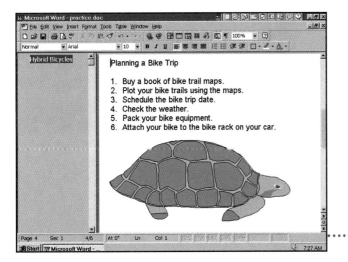

4 In Online Layout View, you see the Document Map on the left side of the window. It is a separate pane that you can use to move around your document and track where you are in the document. Use the Document Map scroll bar to move around a document.

5 To return to Normal view, open the **View** menu and choose **Normal**. ■

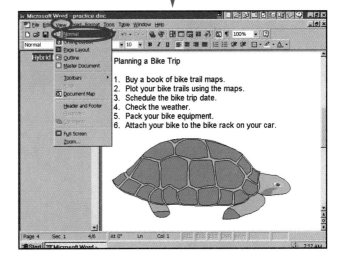

Browsing the Web from Within Microsoft Office

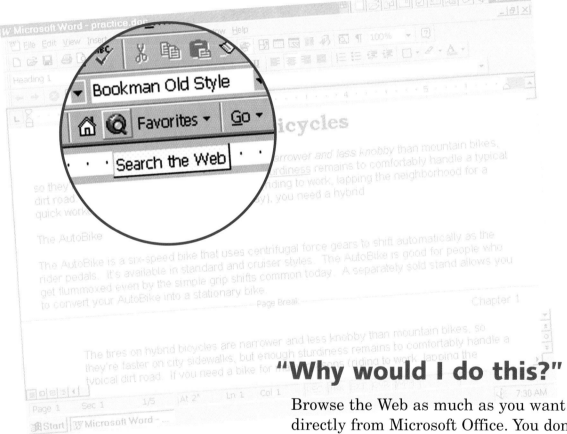

"Why would I do this?"

Browse the Web as much as you want
directly from Microsoft Office. You don't
have to leave the program and start
the Internet Explorer or any other
browser you might normally use. Office
provides a Web toolbar in Word, Excel,
PowerPoint, and Outlook. You can enter
a URL and start searching for a specific
Web page or just browse around the
Web at any time.

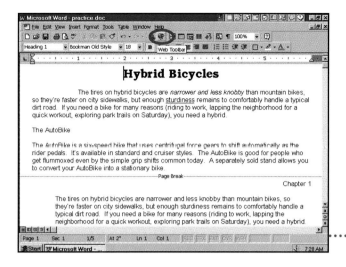

1 In Word, click the **Web Toolbar** button on the Standard toolbar. This displays the Web toolbar.

2 Provide the Web address for which you're searching. Type a URL in the Address text box. For example, enter **www.mcp.com**, which is the URL for Macmillan Computer Publishing.

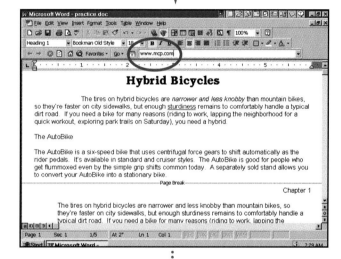

Missing Link

To browse Web pages backward and forward, click the **Back** and **Forward** buttons on the Web toolbar.

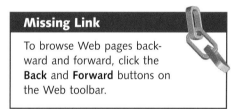

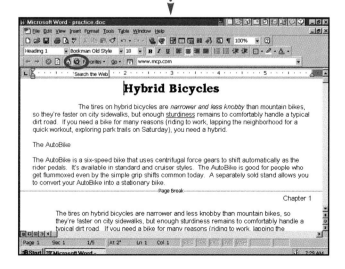

3 Click the **Search the Web** button on the Web toolbar. This searches the Web and displays the Web page you requested. ■

Puzzled?

To reload the current Web page and update it with the latest information, click the **Refresh Current Page** button on the Web toolbar.

TASK 78

Going to a Contact's World Wide Web Page

"Why would I do this?"

Suppose one of your business contacts whom you entered in Microsoft Outlook's Contacts list has a Web page on the Internet. You can view that Web page using Microsoft Office, as long as the contact's information contains an Internet address.

1 Start Outlook as described in Task 1: "Starting and Exiting Microsoft Office 97 Programs." Click the **Contacts** button on the Outlook toolbar. Outlook displays the Contacts View.

2 Double-click a contact in the Contacts list to view the contact's information. That information appears in a dialog box.

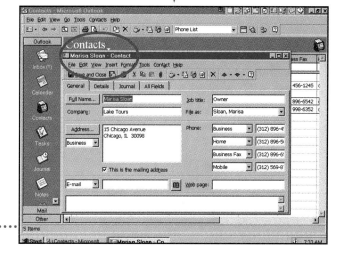

3 To specify the Web Page address that you want to locate, type the contact's URL address in the **Web Page** text box.

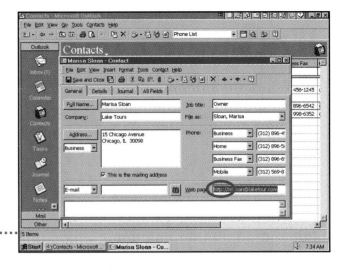

4 Open the **File** menu and choose **Save** to save the Web Page address with the contact's information. Office inserts "http://" in front of the Web Page address. Http is the protocol information that the Web uses to search and locate addresses.

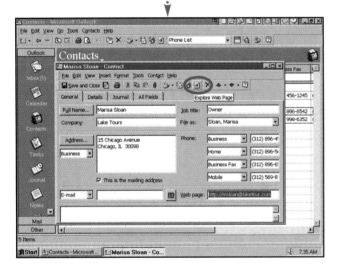

5 Click the **Explore Web Page** button on the Contacts toolbar. This brings you out to the Web, searches for the contact's Web page, and then displays it. ■

Index

Symbols

Index

Index

J-K

journal (Outlook), defined, 251
Journal dialog box (Outlook), 275
journals (Outlook), creating, 274-276
justification, defined, 87
Justify button, Formatting toolbar (Word), 87

L

Last Tab button, tab scrolling buttons, 135
layout of slides (PowerPoint), changing, 227-229
left alignment, defined, 87
lists
    bulleted/numbered, creating in Word documents, 99-102
    contacts list, creating in Outlook, 271-273
    formatting, Excel, 186
locating, *see* finding

M

macro sheets (Excel), defined, 128
magnifying, Zoom Control, 119
Mail button, Outlook toolbar, 254
managing, Outlook Inbox, 252-255
margins, setting in Word documents, 103-105
marquee, defined, 150
Meeting dialog box (Outlook), 264
Meeting Planner (Outlook), 263-265
menu bar, defined, 13
menu commands, selecting, 16-17
menus, closing, 17
Message dialog box (Outlook), 254
messages (Outlook)
    creating, 255
    sending, 255
    viewing, 254
Microsoft Clip Art Gallery dialog box
    PowerPoint, 231
    Word, 111-112

Microsoft Office
    browsing the Web, 292-293
    copying/pasting between programs, 44-47
    creating hyperlinks between documents, 48-50
    exiting, 15
    installing, 12
    starting, 14-15
    switching between programs, 42-43
Microsoft Office Shortcut bar, 12
mixed cell references (Excel), defined, 173
Month button, Calendar toolbar (Outlook), 262
mouse pointer, 13
    changing in PowerPoint slide shows, 247
moving
    appointments in Outlook, 258
    cells in Excel, 152-154
    graphics in Word documents, 112
    insertion point, 61
    ranges in Excel, 154
    text in Word documents, 74-76
moving around, *see* navigating

N

navigating
    between worksheets in Excel, 134-135
    scroll arrows (Excel), 131
    scroll box (Excel), 131
    tab split box (Excel), 132
    within Word documents, 54-55
    Word documents, 59-62
    worksheets in Excel, 129-133
New button, Standard toolbar, 22, 36
New Contact button, Office Shortcut bar, 272
New Journal Entry button, Office Shortcut bar, 275
New Mail Message command (Compose menu), Outlook, 255
New Note button, Office Shortcut bar, 278

New Office Document button, Office Shortcut bar, 43
New Office Document dialog box, 43
Next Tab button, tab scrolling buttons, 135
Normal command (View menu), Word, 291
notes (Outlook)
    creating, 277-278
    defined, 251
    deleting, 278
    opening, 278
    resizing, 278
Notes button, Outlook toolbar, 278
Notes Pages View button, View toolbar (PowerPoint), 242
numbered lists, creating in Word documents, 99-102
Numbering button, Formatting toolbar (Word), 102
numbering pages, Word documents, 106-109
numbers, entering in Excel worksheets, 129

O

Office Assistant (help), 23-26
Office Assistant button, Standard toolbar, 24
Office, *see* Microsoft Office
Online Layout View, Word, 289-291
Open button, Standard toolbar, 38
Open dialog box, 38
    finding files, 40-41
open documents, switching between, 36
opening
    files, 37-38
    notes in Outlook, 278
Operator (Excel), 175-177
Outline view (PowerPoint), 216-219,
    text, changing, 220-222
Outline View button, View toolbar (PowerPoint), 217
overwriting
    cells in Excel, 143-145
    text in Word documents, 56-58